INSIGHT INTO

ADDICTION

INSIGHT INTO
ADDICTION

Bill Radmall

Foreword by Steve Motyer

Published 2009 by CWR, Waverley Abbey House, Waverley Lane, Farnham, Surrey GU9 8EP, UK.
Registered Charity No. 294387. Registered Limited Company No. 1990308.

See back of book for list of National Distributors.

Concept development, editing, design and production by CWR

Printed in China by C&C Offset Printing

ISBN: 978-1-85345-505-6

WAVERLEY ABBEY
INSIGHT SERIES

The Waverley Abbey Insight Series has been developed in response to the great need to help people understand and face some key issues that many of us struggle with today. CWR's ministry spans teaching, training and publishing, and this series draws on all of these areas of ministry.

Sourced from material first presented on Insight Days by CWR at their base, Waverley Abbey House, presenters and authors have worked in close co-operation to bring this series together, offering clear insight, teaching and help on a broad range of subjects and issues. Bringing biblical understanding and godly insight, these books are written both for those who help others and those who face these issues themselves.

CONTENTS

FOREWORD

It was with great delight and anticipation that we welcomed Bill Radmall onto the Theology and Counselling team at London School of Theology, in September 2007. Bill works for CWR, but under the partnership arrangement between CWR and London School of Theology (under which our Theology and Counselling course is run), Bill spends most of his time with us in Northwood, training and caring for our students.

Bill's working life as a psychotherapist has led him to specialise in several areas, and one of these is addiction. And as a pastor, Bill has a deep passion to understand how the resources of the gospel can become real for people in the grip of psychological and emotional disorders, like addictions. Here, in this little book, we meet the fruit of Bill's expertise in both areas – both as a psychological therapist of long experience, and as a theologian and minister.

Addictions of many sorts are becoming one of the chief troubles of our age, especially with the easy access to pornography and gambling provided by the internet. For this reason, Bill focuses on these two areas in this Insight book. Many churches and pastors are discovering terrible and growing areas of need among their people.

In fact, many pastors are themselves being pulled into the dreadful abyss of addiction to internet pornography, driven by the stress, loneliness and 'performance anxiety' of their position.

In this most helpful book – full of deeply wise insight between its slim covers – Bill reveals not only the psychological and emotional dynamic of addiction, but also shows how directly the gospel offers hope and a 'new story' for addicts. Let's not treat addicts and addiction as 'out there', a breed apart, people with problems not felt by 'real Christians'. We are all implicated, as Bill shows, because addiction reveals to us what the essence of sin really is – and we are all sinners in need of God's love.

My prayer is that this little book will bring healing and light to many – or at least a step along the road in that direction. Counsellors will be encouraged and stretched by it, pastors enlightened, and people in the grip of addiction will find themselves understood here, and maybe helped along the road to recovery. And my prayer is also that we'll see further writing of this sort from Bill in the years ahead – we need it!

Steve Motyer
Theology and Counselling Course Leader,
London School of Theology
January 2009

INTRODUCTION

The term 'addiction' is used a lot. A person can become addicted to anything from shopping to sex, from narcotics to gambling online. Our culture provides a vast array of choice in the supermarket of addiction. This is not just a phenomenon that affects a small peripheral group of those who meet in musty church halls to declare their addictive behaviour to each other. Nor is this something that just affects those pop stars and celebrities we see falling over in the street or going into rehab yet again. No, this is also about the parish priest who is up until 4am feeding on the pornographic images on his computer screen. This is about the respectable housewife who has become addicted to online gambling and is terrified her husband will discover that she has spent the family's savings on her compulsive addiction. In other words, addiction is rife in our society.

Of course, there is a continuum of addiction; some dabble at the edges, and some are increasingly controlled and even destroyed by it.

Mark Stibbe[1] has pointed out that our society provides a rich breeding ground for addiction, with its avoidance of pain and suffering. There is a new commandment in Western society: 'Thou shalt not suffer or even feel a bit uncomfortable.' There is an institutional denial and even fear of pain which links with a non-acceptance of ageing, death and suffering. Other factors, such as the media and advertising, reinforce this process with quick-fix solutions to everything from debt to facial wrinkles. I think Jung was right when he said that much neurotic suffering is due to the avoidance of legitimate pain.[2] Our culture is not good at engaging with pain. The common response is to flood it with medication, entertainment, drugs, sex or any number of euphoric experiences.

Now, of course, there is nothing new under the sun! I will outline in this book how the issues that drive addiction go all the way back to the start of humanity. However, the availability of mood-altering experiences and substances is now at a level that has never been known before. I will focus particularly on addiction to pornography and gambling. One reason for this is that since the birth of the Internet, both these activities can now be entered into without ever leaving the house. Moreover, I believe the Internet with its almost unlimited boundaries can draw people into addiction at a rate and depth far greater than previously seen. I agree with those who describe Internet pornography as the crack cocaine of sex addiction.

I hope that *Insight into Addiction* will provide a resource for those struggling with an addiction as well as those trying to help them. It is not primarily for the experts, although I hope some of the connections I make in the book will be of interest. I have structured it in four parts, Part 1 exploring the journey into addiction – the journey into slavery. We shall see the pain of physical or emotional deprivation lies at the root. This part will include reference to different approaches to the issues both from a spiritual as well as psychological perspective.

In Part 2, we will explore the nature of addiction, beginning with links between the nature of slavery in a foreign land and the imprisoning effects of addiction. Here I have particularly focused on the growing issues of addiction to gambling and sex addiction, in particular porn on the Internet. I have chosen to focus on these areas as they are becoming increasingly prevalent in contemporary society. In looking at these forms of addiction we will also encounter the key components of all addictions.

Part 3 uses the language of exodus to begin exploring the difficult journey out of addiction towards freedom and the occupying of one's own 'homeland'. Here there is some discussion about how important it is to recover healthy relationships, as well as the neurology of freedom and reviewing the cycle of red flags, reflex, ritual and release and consequence. I have included in this part issues of accountability as well as looking at the importance of a church community that is hospitable rather than fearful in its dealings with addiction.

Part 4 continues this theme of recovery using the motif of 'occupying the land'. Here I will pick up on the theme of telling new stories of truth as opposed to the thoughts and beliefs that can become strongholds of fear and negativity. A person struggling with addiction can make the journey from their old narrative about themselves to a new lived story, and I will use Jesus' encounter with the Samaritan woman at the well in the Gospel of John to explore how new narratives that enable freedom from addiction can be used.

I am informed in my writing by an interest in a narrative approach to recovery and healing. Put simply, this refers to an understanding of how we can often be controlled, even imprisoned, by oppressive stories of failure and hopelessness; to come out of this and into freedom we need stories of hope, possibility and change. I write this on the day that a new president is elected in the United States of America. On a day like today, it certainly feels like the story of hope has opened up the possibility for real change.

I take a Christian approach to the fundamental change needed so that the story of addiction in an individual's life can become the story of freedom. In dying on the cross, Jesus opened up a way for humanity to come to the Father and be reconciled to Him. This is the most fundamental exodus, a journey from death and sin to hope and freedom. Moreover, as Alcoholics Anonymous has long known, this kind of recovery is not based on humankind's solutions. In fact, coming up with purely human-based solutions is often part of the problem in addiction! One of the keys to freedom is a recognition that *we can't save ourselves.* We have always stood in need of a Saviour!

NOTE: At the end of each chapter, there are some ideas for reflective thought, and a prayer. These have been designed for the reader who wants to work through issues of addiction in their own life, but could be adapted to be used when helping someone else, either in a professional capacity or as a friend or accountability partner.

Bill Radmall
December 2008

NOTES

1   Mark Stibbe, *O Brave New Church: Rescuing the Addictive Culture* (London: DLT, 1995).

2   C. Jung, *The Collected Works of C.G. Jung* (Princeton: Princeton University Press, 1989).

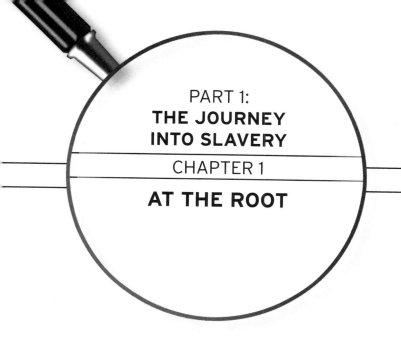

PART 1:
THE JOURNEY INTO SLAVERY

CHAPTER 1

AT THE ROOT

Before we begin to look at the descent into addiction, let us look at the roots of the whole issue – worth a chapter of its own, however short. What are the roots of addiction? The answer can be found in one word: *deprivation*.

These roots can best be understood by looking at them from a biblical, Christian and psychological perspective. Indeed, I do not think we can properly begin to understand the complexity of addiction without taking the integrated approach.

SLAVERY

In the book of Genesis in the Old Testament, we see that the Israelites went to a place that was not their own land because they were starving in the land of their parents.

> When Jacob learned that there was grain in Egypt, he said … 'Go down there and buy some for us, so that we may live and not die.' (Gen. 42:1–2)

The Israelites were filled with fear, faced with the real prospect of being annihilated. There must have been a moment when people realised that they had run out of options, and terror really struck them. They were going to be deprived of the most basic of human needs, the need for food. And there, I believe, is the key word: *deprived*.

For the Israelites, this deprivation was the physical drying up of their food supply but deprivation is so much more than physical deprivation. It would have seemed that the source of life had left them naked and exposed to imminent death, so the Israelites sought out help from neighbouring Egypt.

They eventually moved off their own land and into Egypt, but although under Joseph this was a land of provision, it became a place of slavery.

I believe that at the root of addiction is this same profound sense of abandonment and deprivation. This undermines the three fundamental needs of any human being: security, self-esteem and significance. All these become threatened by the famine in the land. The response of the Israelites is probably the same one we would have in similar circumstances – to start looking around for alternative sources of food, of life. Surely anything is better than nothing! This impulse often lies at the heart of a person's descent into addiction; whatever seems to provide that sense of security, self-esteem and significance can become the drug of choice for the individual addict.

ACTIVITY

Think about a time when you have witnessed real deprivation, even if this is through the media. Write down three words that express, for you, the feelings you experienced.

REFLECTION

• In this first, short, chapter we have discovered that the roots of addiction are to be found in deprivation. The *Concise Oxford English Dictionary* describes the word 'deprivation' as 'the damaging lack of basic material benefits' and 'the lack or denial of something considered essential'.[1] What are the images in your own mind when you think about this whole issue – Third World famine, poverty, want, or something closer to home?

• Why do you think deprivation can result in sheer terror?

• 'Anything is better than nothing'. Is it? Why/why not?

PRAYER

Lord God, as I start this journey into learning about addiction and freedom, please guide, comfort and be with me. In Jesus' precious name I pray. Amen.

NOTE

1   *Concise Oxford English Dictionary* (Oxford: Oxford University Press, 2004).

CHAPTER 2

THE CHRISTIAN PERSPECTIVE

As Christians, we believe that we are born with the desire for God, and yet we tend to displace our longing for God onto other things. This isn't just something that people with addictions do; it's something that we all have a tendency to do.

So, from a Christian point of view, why *do* people get addicted? I believe it is possible to separate the psychological from the theological here, although there are huge overlaps between the two. We will look at the theological implications.

For Christians, the key issue is one of relationship. We see in Genesis 1 and 2 that humankind was made for relationship with the Creator God. Moreover, they were created in the image of a Trinitarian God – Father, Son and Holy Spirit. This means that at the heart of the human DNA is a need for relationship.

THE EFFECTS OF THE FALL

A foundation of being human is this ability to relate to others. This relationality extends across the vertical plane between us and God but also horizontally, between humans. The experience of secure attachment to God was ruptured at the Fall (see Gen. 3) when a decision was taken not to trust the ultimate caregiver. This turning away was also a turning into non-relationship, or a vacuum in relationship. The rupture was played out in Adam blaming Eve for his eating of the fruit from the tree of the knowledge of good and evil (Gen. 3:12). So we can see from this that the breakdown in the relationship between God and humanity was reflected in a breakdown in the relationship between Adam and Eve; in addition, there was a breakdown in the relationship of human beings *with themselves*.

The Fall marks the point at which sin enters into the bloodstream of humanity. From a Christian perspective, one way to understand how addiction works is to refer to the process of sin. But what *is* sin? In his book *Sin as Addiction*,[1] Patrick McCormick defines sin in the following way:

- Sin is alienation from God. Sinners have separated themselves from God and in this detachment entered into a state of chaotic hostility towards self, neighbour and the world.
- Sin is a spiral. There is an escalation from small choices that leads to more disastrous choices. Sin is a progression into the dark.
- Sin is a habitual turning away from relationship with God and into a world of the person's own making. This is in essence a turning away from God's love and call.

Willian Lenters[2] describes being addicted as being like a fly caught in a spider's web, franticly buzzing and spinning around but going nowhere. Augustine concluded that people give up their freedom because it feels good. Part of the thrill may be knowing that the activity being engaged with is wrong; part of sin is the revelling in consciously doing wrong. There could be an addiction to the guilt, wrongness and perversity of the experience. Overwhelming guilt could even become part of an intoxicating cocktail of feelings in the addict. The guilt is then medicated by more acting out.

Human freedom is actually an unseating of God from His throne. In place of His 'rules' we have to come up with our own – but the freedom leads to fear, shame, isolation. Addiction is a turning away from relationship with God and others into a relationship with one's own physical and emotional experience. It may seem as if this turning away from the source of life offers freedom from restriction and control. However, the reality is that this is a turning away from relationship with others towards non-being and alienation. This kind of absolute freedom is the freedom of a person stepping off the edge of a cliff in order to fly, to 'do it their way'. The problem is that this free space is rather like outer space where there is no air. Addicts realise they are unable to breathe. As despair comes closer they panic and grab hold of anything, any substance, any person, any experience which gives them a feeling of reconnecting. In other words, anything that offers them breath.

This describes a vicious and absolute grasping for absolute freedom rather than receiving the freedom that's given by being in relationship with God – this is sin. A key facet of sin is over-reliance upon sensory experience, as if this provided the only sense of reality. The sensual person leads with their body – decisions are decided by the body, not the mind (see Eph. 4:17–19).

So, at this point, the black hole of non-relationship, or relationship with nothing, opened up in humanity's soul. This is described using terms such as 'nothingness', 'emptiness' or a 'dull ache'. Jeff Cook[3] describes evil as holes in God's good creation, decay in places where life is absent.

This empty space where there should be relationship is very difficult to tolerate, and the natural tendency is to fill this gap with 'something'; even if the 'something' that is used produces pain, this is preferable to emptiness. Those who self-harm by cutting themselves often report that they feel more alive when they hurt themselves, and that this is better than the numbness they otherwise feel. I believe there is a close link between this kind of self-harming and addiction.

Separation from relationship with God, others and oneself is impossible to bear. The experience of separation from God is such a catastrophic loss that it triggers paralysing fear in humanity. It is at this point that the terror of death or annihilation enters in – a profound sense of non-being that cannot be integrated into the person's consciousness. This in turn causes God and relationship itself to be feared. So humanity turns away from the domain of relationships and instead turns in on itself, looking inward for comfort. This turning inward could be given as a definition of sin. In this turning, there is an avoidance of truth and reality as defences are erected.

Dallas Willard[4] also notes that there is in this reaction a reversal of the natural hierarchy of a human being. In line with the work of Selwyn Hughes[5] he describes the spiritual aspect of a person as being the 'highest' facility that, through relationship with God, acts as an executive to the mind and body. In addiction and the 'fallen' state of humanity, there is a reversal, with the bodily sensations or highs being experienced rather than the spiritual as the primary source of security, self-esteem and significance. This means that primary needs are addressed in the very inconsistent and unreliable realm of bodily experience rather than in the One in whom 'all things hold together' (Col. 1:17).

SECURITY – IDOLATRY

In essence, because humanity's primary source of attachment is ruptured, people form attachments with alternative objects that they generate or find themselves. This is a profound and insane assertion of self over God. In effect, a person creates a god out of their own experience – out of what they think they can control. This is insane because the reality is that they are handing their souls over to a narcotic experience which, far from being under their own control, in fact controls *them*. The illusion of being God and in control triggers massive anxiety because it is an illusion that needs constant work to maintain. It is a burden that humanity cannot possibly carry. This is why in Alcoholics Anonymous, the first step of their recovery programme is to acknowledge that 'I am powerless over my addiction'. When people become addicts they have had to anaesthetise and blank out anything in their lives that threatens that illusion.

Objects of attachment provide a sense of security. In the Bible, this is described as idolatry. Initially, these idols seem to provide the longed-for security – an example of this in the Old Testament is the Canaanite fertility gods, the Baals and Ashtoreth. These gods seemed to offer the security that a primarily agrarian society needed. However, these gods were demanding and, in worshipping them, the Israelites compromised their sexual purity in orgies with prostitutes attached to the shrines of Baal. Links have been made between these pagan forms of worship centred on the sexual organs, and the problems of pornography addiction. As well as the deterioration of morals, this kind of dependency also results in the person becoming like the thing they worship and are attached to. Given that these idols are essentially empty and human-made, often using wood or stone, those who depend on them themselves develop wooden or stony hearts. Once again, there is a link here with the experience of addicts whose sensitivity to their own and others' feelings becomes numbed. The further the addiction erodes a person's life, the more anaesthetised they become to their own feelings and those of others around them. This is why often relatives and friends of the addict describe them as being selfish or narcissistic, with limited awareness of others' needs. I believe this correlates with the hardness of heart referred to, for example, in Ezekiel (see 11:19; 36:26).

The question could be asked that if humankind without God is prone to potentially addictive self-comfort, then why isn't everyone an addict? This leads us to the psychological roots of addiction.

ACTIVITY
Flick through the pages of a magazine or newspaper, and spend some time identifying as many modern-day 'idols' as you can.

REFLECTION
- What makes you feel secure, full of self-worth and significance? Be honest!
- Can you identify any idols in your life?
- Sin, separation from God, leads to the terrible bleakness of non-

relationship. This in turn can lead us to fill the vacuum with 'gods' of our own making. Then we are in danger of becoming like our 'gods'. If this is a description of your own life (or the life of someone you know and are trying to help) you may wish to share some of your feelings with a trusted friend or counsellor as you begin your own personal journey through this book.

PRAYER

Loving Father God, I thank You that You so desire relationship with me, Your child. You have provided a wonderful way back to You, when Your only Son died on the cross so that I might be forgiven for all my sin, and be restored to You. Thank You that You love me so much. Amen.

NOTES

1 Patrick McCormick, *Sin as Addiction* (New Jersey: Paulist Press, 1989).
2 William Lenters, *The Freedom We Crave* (Grand Rapids: Eerdmans, 1985).
3 Jeff Cook, *Seven: The Deadly Sins and the Beatitudes* (Grand Rapids: Zondervan, 2008).
4 Dallas Willard, *Renovation of the Heart* (Colorado Springs: NavPress, 2002).
5 Selwyn Hughes, *Christ Empowered Living* (Surrey: CWR, 2002).

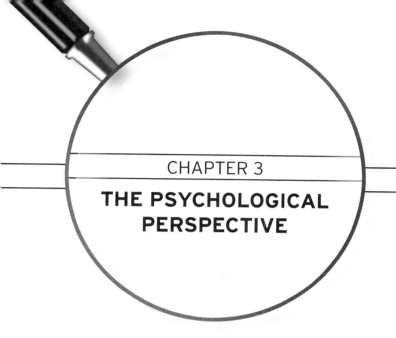

CHAPTER 3

THE PSYCHOLOGICAL PERSPECTIVE

In my experience, working as a psychotherapist, the main thing I keep coming up against in people with addictions is a tremendous *clutching or grasping anxiety.*

BACKGROUNDS

There is a sort of quality to this anxiety which is like a small child who has been left, but not left for quite so long that they have shut down; they are still clinging on; in a sense, it does not really matter what they grab hold of as long as they grab hold of *something.* If you talk to them about it, they will describe a feeling that if they don't do something immediately to quell those feelings, they will fall into an empty nothingness. If you ask them to describe what's inside them, they might say, 'Nothing – just a gaping kind of emptiness.' There is a sense in addictions that nothing is ever enough – however much the addict gets, it's *never* enough.

There is a move these days away from the kind of parent-blaming culture we had in the 1960s and 1970s where everything was caused by bad parenting. We are more aware that traumas in school life or through bullying or peer pressure can affect people in their teenage years. But I would have to say, from my experience, that the majority of people with addictions seem to have had troubled backgrounds in terms of their family life, usually characterised by insecure, broken or non-existent attachment to their caregivers in the early years of their lives.

A child may have grown up in a family where perhaps one of the parents was an alcoholic. The whole family may have tiptoed around the alcoholic for years because they didn't want to make things worse. Any strong feelings had to be suppressed because if anyone said anything and it upset the alcoholic, they would go crazy – and then the person who'd spoken out would be blamed.

This kind of family atmosphere creates a background where children grow up learning to suppress all their feelings, not saying anything that will be upsetting, believing the best way to deal with stress would be to take a drug. So they may eventually come to therapy in incredible distress with an out of control addiction, not knowing how to deal with it.

LEGITIMATE NEEDS

There is often a need in addicts to be the 'good boy' or 'good girl'. Often addicts will grow up in families where it is not acceptable to be bad or messy or naughty and will learn to develop a false self which is quite compliant and good, people-pleasing and maybe looking after others. And so when their addiction does come to light, it is often a terrible shock for those around them, because it is the last thing that they thought somebody 'like that' would be doing. They were such a kind, gentle person – why is it that they are now looking at pornography on the Internet every hour of the night? How did that happen?

So addicts have deep legitimate needs for security, love and comfort – just like the rest of us – that by and large have probably not been met for whatever reason, and so they look for that comfort in illegitimate ways, ways that are actually destructive to them. The truth is that only God can be the Bread of Life to them. Therefore, it's certainly worth bearing in mind when we are talking to people with addictions that they have the same needs as everybody else. Although they may be messing their lives up by meeting their needs in destructive ways, we should remember that their needs are quite legitimate but they have just not been met though the course of their lives – through some form of a breakdown in relationship, probably with key caregivers.

RESTLESS HEART

I have suggested that from a Christian perspective the whole of humanity has a problem. This problem stems from a rupturing of relationship to the most secure base for existence there is – God. But ask people on the street, and it is unlikely that many would acknowledge that they have a gaping chasm inside them. People do not generally describe a God-shaped hole in their lives that they are seeking to fill. They may only be aware of an undefined dissatisfaction. However, this doesn't mean the need isn't there. What it probably does mean is:

- *The person has defended themselves from any awareness of their emptiness* – perhaps by not allowing any time to think or reflect on their lives. I recently conducted a funeral in my capacity as a minister. I was invited back to the home of the deceased for a gathering of family and friends, during which I was very struck by the fear and anxiety being expressed in several conversations. The core of what was being expressed was: 'You never really think about your life until something like this happens.' I believe that what was being brought to awareness was the fear of death, which for many is the ultimate separation from relationship with anything or anyone. In Western society this is a taboo that is often avoided. So people on the street could just be filling their lives with so much activity that they keep their awareness of issues of mortality and existential emptiness at bay.

- *The person may already be medicating and anaesthetising their emptiness with activity (workaholism), food, TV, religiosity (excessive and all-consuming church commitments) or a drink after work.* These and many other similar activities may not be causing any clear problems in the person's life and relationships; therefore, although the person is somewhat dependent on these activities for security, self-esteem or significance, they would not identify their behaviour as addictive. Although I have no way of proving it, I suspect that the majority of the population may fall into this category!

There is a third kind of person, too:

- *Those who may* well *be aware of their anxieties/loneliness, are quite self-aware and switched on to their feelings. But they don't try to fill the vacuum with addictions.* The crucial difference, and the key to these people not falling into addiction, is twofold. Firstly, if there is a genetic predisposition to addiction, they don't have it. Secondly, they have an ability not only to

identify their feelings but are able to regu⌐
their emotions without relying on external quic⌐
whether these be narcotics or masturbation and p⌐

Let's take a closer look at this third category. From a C⌐   ⌐an
perspective, these people still need Jesus and are still suffering the
existential alienation of those in the other two categories. From a
psychological perspective, they find other ways of managing their
emotional lives without recourse to the false comfort and strength
of an addiction. I would suggest that these people may have been
securely attached to their primary caregivers.

THE PRIMARY CAREGIVER

The role of the primary caregiver is to enable the infant to process
their emotions. This process begins with the parent having space
in their own minds to identify the infant's emotional state. The
parents accepting and sensitive reactions to the infant enable the
infant to in turn identify and process their own feelings. However,
if the parent does not supply this kind of secure base for the infant
child to attach to, the infant's stress levels may increase. This
is also likely to happen if the parent is emotionally absent, for
example because of illness, preoccupation with their own stresses
such as finance, relationship difficulties or their own addictions.
At the other extreme, parents may be too intrusive, breaking the
boundaries of their children. This happens in cases of sexual,
emotional or physical abuse. Once again, the infant's stress levels
are raised. At the neurological level, an increase in stress will make
it more difficult for the infant to regulate their feelings. Without
a safe, containing relationship with their primary caregivers
an infant may not feel safe or confident enough to face painful

feelings. If they do not have the relationship with caregivers that facilitates a working through of difficult feelings they may be prone to cutting off and repressing them. Feelings become something to fear, as they represent an unmanageable level of distress, anxiety or pain. This can lead to a two-way process that in turn provides fertile ground for the establishment of addictions.

PATTERNS

Firstly, a pattern of avoidance of anything that triggers anxiety is formed. This means that rather than anxiety being tolerated and worked through as part of the process of growth and development, it is avoided. This can have the effect of freezing the person at a stage of development. They can go no further because their anxiety prevents them.

The second pattern that feeds directly into addictions is that the person seeks to regulate their anxiety not through using their own resources, but by leaning on external sources of comfort and regulation. These things often provide an experience of pleasure and euphoria. As we shall discover later on, there is usually a process or cycle of addiction that may go on for hours or even days. It is not just about the moment that the drug of choice is experienced. Addicts can become quite euphoric even in the phase of the addictive cycle when they are anticipating acting out. The acting out itself is often the final part of this process. The feeling of euphoria that the false comfort provides will have the effect of detaching the addict from all their feelings of anxiety and discomfort. This may be only a momentary release, but for that moment they feel attached to something; they feel saved and safe. The rush of opiates in the brain at that moment literally acts as a painkiller and, to this extent, addiction works. The problem is that because these euphoric moments negate and anaesthetise emotional pain, the addict never has the opportunity to improve their management of feelings. It is rather like a child in school who keeps getting another child to do their homework for them. They never learn their subject and they are lost when put under exam stress. While the addict is acting out they cannot improve their 'score' at dealing with stress. Unfortunately, this avoidance often gets worse; the person's tolerance of stress gets less and less and their need to use their drug of choice just to manage gets more and more. This is the effect sometimes described as 'tolerance'.

Neurologically, the addict's repeated ways of behaving become patterns that the brain naturally and easily falls into. This could be described rather like the way that grooves are cut in a vinyl record. The needle will naturally fall into these grooves, and likewise, the mind under stress will fall into the grooves of addiction. This makes getting out of the addictive process seem both counter-intuitive, but also very uncomfortable, for the recovering addict.

So, what is happening in the addict's mind is that the part that feels emotion becomes disconnected from the part that more consciously processes it. This means that the person is often unable to identify what they are feeling, and any feeling is interpreted as a threat to be avoided. This has serious repercussions for relationships. Those in close relationship to the addict often feel as if they are cut off from the person at an emotional level. For this reason, addicts often find intimacy with a partner threatening and overwhelming. This is particularly true of sex addicts who retreat into a self-made world that replaces emotional intimacy with sexual highs.

Another reason that relationships are difficult for addicts is that they generally fear losing control. Any loss of control threatens to upset the emotional knife-edge upon which they balance so precariously. One of the defining features of any relationship, whether with God or a human being, is that you cannot control the other person's thoughts, feelings and reactions. Again this can be experienced as threatening to the addict.

ACTIVITY

Bread is a staple part of our diet. Read about Jesus, the Bread of Life, in John 6:25–59. What does it mean for Jesus to be bread for us?

REFLECTION

- Addicts have deep legitimate needs for security, love and comfort – just like everyone else. It is just that they look for that comfort in illegitimate ways; ways that are actually destructive to them. Meditate on that fact for a little while.
- Do you have a 'restless heart'?
- Are you avoiding issues which cause stress, or dealing with anxiety by leaning on external sources? Be aware that Jesus can be the Bread of Life for you today.

PRAYER

Lord, thank You that You understand and accept me. You know what drives me, You know why I am as I am. I thank You that in You is freedom. You are the answer to all my needs. Thank You for Your presence as I continue on my journey to freedom from addiction. Amen.

PART 2:
LIFE IN EGYPT

CHAPTER 4

WHAT IS ADDICTION?

As we return to the book of Genesis, we see that chapter 50 finds Joseph and his family still in Egypt: 'Joseph stayed in Egypt, along with all his father's family' (Gen. 50:22). Presumably the famine is over, but they have remained. Perhaps they have become comfortable in this foreign land, even though it is not what God had promised them. Joseph knows this and his dying wish is to be taken back to the promised land, the land where Israel would return to its place in God's plans (see Gen. 50:24–25).

CONSEQUENCES
In the slow decline into addiction, the addict is not initially aware that they are becoming dependent on their drug of choice. This has been described as being rather similar to a frog being boiled alive. If the water is cold at first, and then the heat is gently turned up, the frog is not aware of the danger until it is too late.

Neurologically, the brain at the deep level of the limbic centre adjusts to whichever object gives comfort and a reduction of stress. This has far-reaching consequences:

1. The core experience of pain is not faced.
2. Stress can trigger the pain which, because it's stored in the limbic system, has the same intensity it had at the beginning.
3. The individual lives increasingly inside the apparent safety that their false comfort offers.
4. The person fears revealing their true self to anyone because they hold a core belief/lie that they are unlovable. This leads to developing a false self, like an Israelite living on foreign soil as if they were an Egyptian.
5. The false self may seem arrogant – apparently not needing others – distant.
6. The avoidance of pain, and need for self-comfort distorts the person's relationship with themselves. They forget who they are. They lose touch with the 'land' of their own bodies. They become insensitive to their own emotional feeling and the feelings of others: 'Having lost all sensitivity, they have given themselves over to sensuality so as to indulge in every kind of impurity, with a continual lust for more' (Eph. 4:19).

Joseph was embalmed and placed in a coffin in Egypt. Living in perpetual exile from oneself is a form of death, even if it comes from an understandable attempt to stave off annihilation.

That is part of the nature of addiction: those with it tend to compartmentalise their life so that on one level they are just living the average everyday life, and on another level they are living a completely separate life that nobody knows anything about.

So it's quite easy in some ways for an addict to get deeper and deeper into their cycle without anybody knowing about it until things have got quite seriously out of hand. Hidden, shameful ways of dealing with feelings of pain, sadness, anger and sorrow that can't be expressed in relationship with others come out in a 'split off' aspect of the person's life, in whatever their addiction is. Some will be more obvious than others: overeating, for example, leading to weight gain is perhaps more noticeable than other addictions. Alcoholism often isn't obvious, and it's very rare statistically for people to be falling down in the street drunk before anybody notices; actually, I would say there is a gender divide there. It tends to be better hidden in women, and doesn't always seem to come to light so quickly. In any case, it is a hidden aspect of any person's life.

The other thing that happens as addiction gets deeper in somebody is that their tolerance for the buzz of the addiction goes up, so they need to do more and more to get the same buzz they had when they began. This leads to an escalation of their behaviour to get the same effect. So, for example somebody who may have started off scratching their arm with their fingernails to get relief from their pain might, a few months down the line, need to cut deep gashes in their arms with a knife to get the same effect. Therefore, we can see that there is a dangerous escalation aspect to addiction.

DEFINITION OF ADDICTION

Addiction is a dependency on a mood-altering experience or substance. This dependency is to some degree physical as well as emotional. The addictive experience, the high, provides the addict with a euphoric release (however temporary) from pain.

This pain is characterised by fear, stress and anxiety. When in the grip of their addictive cycle the addict's behaviour, thinking and feeling is solely focused on achieving their high. This causes an almost trancelike state in which their awareness of other people, their own morality, possible consequences and, most significantly, their pain, ceases to exist. The end of this cycle is always marked with remorse and self-hatred.

The mood-altering experience is created by a flood of opiates being released in the brain from within the person. These are not necessarily a result of ingesting narcotics. Often an experience can trigger the pleasure centre of the brain. So a shopaholic hitting the shopping mall may neurologically experience a similar opiate high to a drug user. The activities and experiences that trigger this reaction are vast: they can range from pornography to food, romantic fantasy to chocolate, heroin to alcohol, online gambling to shopping, self-harming (for example, cutting) to playing computer games, acquiring money or fame to achieving the approval of others ... the list could go on.

Addicts can be *addicted* to stress, strangely enough, and I think these days there are a lot of people who go from stress situation to stress situation, perhaps as workaholics, who have actually got into an addictive cycle that they can't get out of. The way to know that it's an addiction is if you are trying to help someone stop whatever they are doing but they are not able to because they are addicted to the thing they are stressed about. For instance, a workaholic would usually find it impossible to stop thinking about work even if they were to go on holiday.

This definition focuses on the individual's experience, and this is important because addiction is a deeply solitary and individualistic process. Even for those addicted to sex with others the experience is still about what 'I' want, and in a sense the other person only exists as an object to serve 'my needs'. The consequences for relationships can be corrosive and catastrophic. A key feature of addiction is that the addict retreats into a world of their own making and finds intimacy with others awkward, uncomfortable or threatening. Those close to an addict may feel a distance opening up in the relationship. The other person may seem preoccupied. They may be more irritable, particularly if questioned or challenged. There may be periods of time when they cannot account for their whereabouts or seem to be covering up. They may be increasingly secretive and defensive. What can be particularly confusing is that sometimes the addict may seem very positive and loving, perhaps making grand gestures such as giving a lavish gift or being particularly loving. This may be either because they are high or that they are feeling remorseful after acting out, and want to make amends. It could also be that they are making a 'new start' and have resolved to be good. Unfortunately these resolutions are usually short-lived and quickly broken. This can then trigger a resurgence of self-loathing and depression that is hard for partners and loved ones to understand. Particularly in the case of those involved with sex addicts, they may feel quite used and objectified in the sexual aspect of their relationship. The addict partner may demand sex but be unable to offer intimacy. All these processes can be destructive to the self-esteem and confidence of those close to them. This is one reason that groups such as Alcoholics Anonymous exist, to support the families and relatives of addicts – because they are just as impacted by the addiction as the addict.

Don Williams says that addiction is 'Desire gone amuck. Rather than being nailed to God it is nailed to other gods'.[1] That highlights the key issue in addiction, which is that desire has become attached to something that is less than God.

Addiction affects us in various ways. It affects us biologically, physiologically, psychologically and spiritually. Whatever else an addiction does, it affects the way we think. It affects the way we feel, and that includes the chemistry of our brains; so when we are in the grip of an addiction, the brain chemistry actually changes and the brain gets used to these sorts of bursts of adrenalin and energy that happen in addiction. I previously used the illustration of a vinyl record, with the grooves cut into it; it is worth reiterating here that this is what happens to the brain over time – grooves get cut and embedded into the brain's neural pathways, so that we actually feel more normal if we are an addict doing our addiction than we would the rest of the time. In effect, the addict doing their addiction is doing what comes most naturally to them, from a neurological point of view as well as an emotional or psychological point of view.

THE SPIRITUAL VIEW

From a spiritual viewpoint, Don Williams' definition is quite useful because it highlights that really we are meant to desire God; we are meant to be turned towards God. Leanne Payne describes being 'focused on the upward movement of our lives towards our Creator rather than being bent towards the created'[2], and the whole thrust of addiction is that it is very much a turning away from the Creator, and towards something that is created that gives us a quick fix.

Addiction is a soul-destroying slow death in which the sufferer loses touch with the reality of who they are, who God is, and the world around them. It's characterised by deception, shame and an escalating loss of control. At its worst, addicts may become reclusive and stop looking after themselves as they sink into the oblivion of being totally abandoned to their drug of choice. Conversely, they may only have the odd slip-up now and again. This does not mean they are not an addict, it might just mean that their cycle of addiction is longer. So, for example, somebody who is addicted to something such as overeating may go on a binge at the beginning of the month and not do it again for another two months, and yet they may still be addicted to binge eating. It just means that they were not under the right stress in those two months to do it again; however, if they were under a lot of stress for the whole two months they might do it more frequently. It sometimes just depends on what kind of stress the person is under as to how many times they do their addictive behaviour.

From a Christian perspective, some may ask whether a better way of describing addiction is just 'a loss of self-control'. There may be suspiciousness of terms such as 'sex addiction' or 'food addiction'. Some Christians may discount the idea of pathological addiction and prefer to describe these patterns of thought, behaviour and feeling as lust or gluttony. This perspective translates the word 'addiction' into various sins. I would not dispute that there is something about addiction that draws the sufferer away from God. However, it needs to be understood that from the sufferer's point of view, they feel overtaken by forces beyond their control. They are in the grip of terrible compulsions that can seem irresistible.

For anyone attempting to help a person who is addicted, or for the addicted one themselves, there is a need to go beyond the knowledge that what they are doing is wrong and into a deeper understanding of *why* they have become addicted in the first place. It seems unlikely that any attempt to help the addict will be successful without some insight into what creates the nightmare of addiction. There are key patterns that can be found in the behaviour, thinking and feelings of those who are addicted. I suggest that no matter what the actual focus of a person's addiction is, the cycle of an addiction is nevertheless similar.

PAIN AVOIDANCE

It's a natural human trait that we want to avoid pain and attach ourselves to pleasurable objects. So people who have been in pain tend to crowd out whatever painful feelings they have had, or are having, by seeking pleasure in some form. Pleasure is rewarding because it does actually work; it does displace pain and reduces stress.

So what could this pain be that people with addiction are trying to manage? Well, lots of things! It could be a profound sense of isolation and loneliness if there has been abandonment, especially if this happened when the person was young. It could be fears, anxieties, self-hatred, inadequacy and shame. There are so many different causes of pain in people! I don't agree with a lot of things that Jung said, but one of the things I do agree with is that all neurosis is caused by the avoidance of legitimate pain.[3] All neurosis and addictions would fall into this category.

We certainly live in a society which goes to great lengths to avoid pain, in the form of grief and loss in particular. We've got a pill for everything – we have an idea that we can get rid of any sort of trouble with pharmaceutical help, and we live in a very, very pain-averse society. So it is no surprise that people grow up expecting to be able to find some way of getting out of anything that makes them feel stressed or in pain – and of course many people's lives *are* painful. Many children are growing up today with maybe severe trauma in their family – a lot of chaos going on at home – and that will come out in pain that they will try to manage in some way or another. There is certainly a big upswing in things like self-harming now, among girls especially, but also among boys; certainly an upswing in drink, and abuse of alcohol in schools as well.

THE ADDICTIVE PROCESS

The addictive process, or cycle, is a recurring pattern that addicts keep going round and round in. Part of the treatment for addiction is to identify what the person's cycle is: How does it start? What do they do? What happens afterwards?

RED FLAGS

The first part of the addictive cycle is commonly described as 'Red flags'. Red flags are moments where something triggers the addict – it will be different for different people. For example, if the thing that particularly causes someone to be stressed and then to go for their addiction is being alone, then that would be their red flag. When the red flag starts, it triggers off a sort of preoccupation; they start thinking about doing the thing that they want to do. For someone who is a shopaholic, it might be that they start thinking about going out and buying something. It's usually triggered by pain or the prospect of feeling pain, so a typical example would be this: A shopaholic has got a job interview, and they are feeling stressed about it; they don't want to make a fool of themselves. Their particular 'thing' might be that they are frightened that people won't like them. If they have low self-esteem, they might fear that people will reject them, so for them that could be a red flag. This is a dangerous situation for them to be in. They will start thinking about going out shopping just before they go to the interview; that will make them feel a bit better and just take the edge off their anxiety. So they go to the shopping mall and into the stores and, before they know it, time has gone by because they have got so absorbed in the thing they were looking to buy. The interview is long gone, but in a way they feel better because they are not feeling stressed any more; they feel happier than they did. So it worked! And that is the whole thing with addictions – people wouldn't do it if they didn't find that it worked.

Addictions are extremely effective in terms of helping to blank out bad feelings, and to bring up some good feelings even if the addict feels bad afterwards.

So that's how red flags work. They are the starting point of the whole cycle and for different people they will have different red flags, different things that trigger them, that stress them particularly, depending on their background and the areas that they are vulnerable in.

REFLEX

The second part of the cycle is the 'Reflex'. This is when the person begins to plot what they are going to do next and starts making a few choices. So going back to the shopaholic example, the person might start getting into their car, they might decide to go down the road towards the shopping mall; they will actually start making some choices about what they are going to do. They are not quite there yet but they are on their way; they have started the journey.

RITUAL

The third aspect is the 'Ritual'. This encompasses the whole journey between the first impulse and the final destination and because it's a ritual, it's something that is repeated and repeated and repeated.

If we think of somebody who is a pornography addict, they will often go to the same newsagents to get the pornography, parking in the same place, maybe at the same time of day – it will all be very ritualised; the whole thing is like a repeated cycle. While they are doing this, the person is often in a kind of foggy euphoria, feeling quite good in a way because, by this stage, they have started to leave responsibility behind. The stressful feelings are going down because they are so preoccupied with what they are going towards. One person has described it as 'one's whole being pulsing with carnal anticipation', which is quite a good description, I think. It's almost impossible to slow down or stop – all that matters is the object of the desire. So this is like an arrow that has been fired at a target – it has already left the bow and is halfway towards it.

RELEASE AND CONSEQUENCE

The final part of the sequence is 'Release and consequence'. At some point there will be a kind of ecstatic release – whether it's winning money when gambling online or whatever it is – there will be a moment of adrenalin rush and feeling good, but it's often followed by numbness, guilt, shame and an aching emptiness. The problem with that is that those are the very feelings that can trigger off another cycle, so typically a person will feel dreadful after they have done whatever they have done. They probably didn't really want to do it; it certainly isn't something they are proud of, and they start beating themselves up about it, feeling bad, feeling 'Oh, I always do this kind of thing because I am just a rubbish person'. They start playing out the old tapes at the back of their mind about how rubbish they really are and, before they know it, they feel so bad they need to act out their addictive cycle again. So you can see how this is quite a nasty spiral that can keep repeating back on itself.

NOTE: In the next two chapters, I will focus on gambling and on pornography addiction – in particular, Internet porn. I am focusing on these areas partly because there is much already written on narcotic and alcohol addiction but also because with the massive advances in technology in recent years, there are many opportunities to gamble online and use pornography. These are serious issues that need to be addressed.

ACTIVITY
Read Psalm 139, and then rewrite it in your own words, in the form of a letter from God to you.

REFLECTION
- How is addiction like living 'in Egypt'? Are you living in Egypt?
- 'There is something about addiction that draws the sufferer away from God. However, it needs to be understood that from the sufferer's point of view, they feel overtaken by forces beyond their control.' Know that God can lead you out of your personal Egypt, just as He led the Israelites out of their captivity. Nothing is too hard for Him. You might find it helpful to meditate on the greatness and awesomeness of the God who loves you and knows you intimately.

- Spend some time identifying your own 'Red flags'. Jot them down in a notebook, or perhaps share them with someone you trust.

PRAYER

Father, I thank and praise You because You are showing me such truths about the nature of addiction. Thank You that You are able to lead the addict out of Egypt, for nothing is impossible to You. Thank You for Your great love and compassion. Amen.

NOTES

1   Don Williams, *Jesus and Addiction* (San Diego: Recovery Publications Inc., 1993).
2   Leanne Payne, *Restoring the Christian Soul* (Eastbourne: Kingsway, 1994).
3   Carl Jung, *The Collected Works of C.G Jung* (Princeton: Princeton University Press, 1989).

CHAPTER 5

GAMBLING

The tail end of the twentieth century has seen a big increase in gambling. There has been unprecedented de-regulation of gambling in numerous countries throughout the world.[1]

In the UK, opportunities to gamble are available in most high streets in the form of betting shops, amusement arcades and bingo clubs, as well as in supermarkets, post offices, cafés, pubs, leisure centres and other venues that sell tickets for the National Lottery. There is also the increased use of the Internet.

THE JAMES BOND IMAGE?

The common image of a gambler as some kind of James Bond figure who plays with high rollers in the casinos of Monte Carlo is only a small aspect of the world of gambling. Conversely, gambling now extends far beyond the bookies and race or dog tracks. Like sexuality, it now surfaces in many forms of entertainment media and proliferates on the Internet. In particular, the National Lottery has become associated with the mass entertainment format, with pop stars performing, and glossy ad campaigns. Lottery gamblers cut across all sections of society. It is far from unusual to see those who are struggling to pay their bills or buy groceries still 'doing the lottery' in newsagents up and down the land. Winning the lottery has now slipped into cultural mythology as the 'holy grail' – the one thing, the one hope, that will change everything.

None of this means that to take part in these populist forms of gambling equates in any way to an *addiction* to gambling. What it does mean is that many more people now have the opportunity to enter into gambling activity with minimal effort. A lot of early stage gambling is seen as harmless fun or 'just a flutter'. There may be some influence from other gamblers in the family. It is more socially acceptable than porn. For those who are vulnerable to meeting their spiritual and emotional needs in the buzz of a bet or a potential win, this can become a doorway into greater dependency on gambling.

Joe has been a gambler from before he had met his wife, Louise. They have been together for twenty years. He has been getting into ever-increasing debt as a result of his addiction to poker. Then Joe and Louise decide to move house. Louise is excited about making a new start, particularly as Joe has seemed so preoccupied and distracted recently. She hopes this can be a new beginning for their relationship. She has no idea of the seriousness of Joe's gambling or consequent debt. He may have been chasing, which means going back day after day to try and make back the money lost the previous day. This cycle has led to making increasingly poor choices in card games and increasingly reckless bets. On the day they are due to exchange contracts and sell their old house, Louise is contacted by the mortgage lender. She is devastated to hear that the mortgage has not been paid for several months and the house will probably be repossessed. The whole deal to sell up and buy their dream home is in ruins.

When Joe returns from work, Louise has just one question for him – the question those closest to gambling addicts always ask eventually: 'Where has all the money gone?' In Louise's case she also asks, 'And with it, all my dreams for a new life?' Like many other gamblers who are cornered in this way by circumstances, Joe may hit rock bottom. He might confess the full extent of his addiction. He will probably be filled with shame, remorse and self-hatred. He may even be suicidal. On a more positive note, this could also be the moment when he goes for help, perhaps to Gamblers Anonymous. However, the devastation of gambling has implications for the whole family. Trust is eroded and, as with other addictions, relationships will be put under potentially terminal stress. People will risk every part of their life to gamble; this can lead to the breakdown in relationships. The children of the gambler can also be affected; in the course of my work as a counsellor, I have met several children of gamblers who display the same issues with needing to be there for others at the expense of their own needs that children of alcoholics can also express.

The person trying to stop gambling may not be chemically addicted in quite the same way as an alcoholic. However, the high of the anticipation of gambling (and it is often the anticipation, not the bet itself, that creates the 'buzz') still releases opiate-like chemicals into the bloodstream. It's not clear if gamblers have a physical tolerance. It may be that they just need to get bigger wins and risk more money to cover increasing debts. So, when people stop gambling there are, at the very least, psychological withdrawal symptoms. The recovering gambler can also become restless and irritable after stopping gambling. This may be a heightening of the restlessness a gambler exhibits in any case. Stopping gambling may also reveal an underlying depression which as in so many addictions may be being masked or medicated by the euphoric addictive highs.

SWEPT AWAY

Gamblers tend to have the experience of being swept away by forces beyond their control. They may not see themselves as making decisions and choices. Instead it is fate or 'lady luck' or the dice or the horses that their fortunes rest upon. Over time this particular form of addiction erodes any sense of responsibility for one's own life. The control and power seems to be in the hands of other people or circumstances. Not surprisingly this leads to passivity and helplessness. It is this sense of being out of control that triggers anxiety and stress in the gambler. This in turn triggers further gambling in a vain effort to regain control. The paradox, however, is that the very thing the addict uses to regain control takes control further and further out of their hands.

Although the gambler's life can be seriously out of control and chaotic they may give the impression that all is well, even to those who are close to them. They may be very skilled at fabricating elaborate cover-ups for the extent of their debt and addiction. Sometimes these cover-ups are exposed when financial ruin suddenly catches up with the gambler's family. This can in turn lead to further shame and distress and a resurgence of the gambling in order to make things right.

ACTIVITY

Stanley spent all his life doing the football pools, hoping for a big win 'to make life better'. He also loved the lottery, scratch cards, the horses, and the dogs. When he died, his elderly wife admitted he had always kept her short of housekeeping money; she had never had any luxuries. His family had trouble remembering him with any great degree of love or affection. If you had known Stanley, before he discovered the pools and so on, and he had asked you how he could make life better for his family, what would you have told him?

REFLECTION

- Do you have a glamorised, 'James Bond' idea of gambling?
- Do you believe there is any danger in someone 'having a flutter on the horses'? What about prize draws, a game of bingo during a night out with friends?
- Imagine someone who wants to stop doing the National Lottery every week. The trouble is, they use the same numbers week in, week out – what if their numbers come up the very week they stop? How is that like being in bondage or slavery?

PRAYER

Lord Jesus, I thank You that You know the treadmill the gambler is on. You know how one thing leads to another, and how easily everything spirals out of control. I praise You, Lord, that You can set the gambler free. (If you have issues with gambling yourself, or are helping someone caught in gambling addiction, you might like to ask Jesus to come into that situation now.) Amen.

NOTE

1   Much of the material in this chapter is taken from J. Orford et al., *Gambling and Problem Gambling in Britain* (Hove: Brunner-Routledge, 2003).

CHAPTER 6

SEX ADDICTION

The second major addiction that I want to focus on is what is commonly called 'sex addiction'. Until fairly recently this was viewed as an indulgence of the rich and famous. It has sometimes been dismissed as just a modern, and rather clinical, way of describing lust. From a Christian perspective, sex addiction certainly is about lust; however, it is also becoming increasingly recognised that sexual lust can, in itself, become a toxic addiction.

Patrick Carnes[1] has written extensively about the nature of sexual addiction. As with all addictions, this stems from deep-rooted assumptions about oneself.

TOM'S STORY

The story below is fictional, but the details are increasingly the real story for many men. The phenomenon of Internet porn addiction is unfortunately also becoming a problem for some women.

Tom is a successful businessman. He has worked for the same firm of chartered surveyors for twenty years and is a well-respected member of the community. He is one of the elders in his church. Over the last six months, he has been leading the church through an interregnum. Many people have been coming to him with their problems and complaints. He has found this very stressful but not wishing to worry his wife, he has kept his feelings of stress – and even panic – to himself. When he comes home from work, he has just enough time to eat dinner (often alone as his wife, Liz, has eaten with their two teenage children) before he is out again at a church meeting. He has not had a sexual relationship with his wife for a year now. They don't have time to discuss their increasing isolation from one another as she is preoccupied with their son's upcoming exams, and seems very stressed by her job as a part-time teacher. Tom has started staying up late at night on his own after Liz has gone to bed, even though he is exhausted. He may have a few beers and, in recent months, has been becoming increasingly engrossed in the world of pornography available on his laptop computer. He is able to forget his problems as he enters into a euphoric trance that sometimes lasts until dawn. He compulsively masturbates, finding that this activity temporarily relieves his stress. Recently, he has been missing days at work. One day, his wife comes down at breakfast-time to find Tom asleep in front of his computer. She goes to turn the machine off but, as she touches the screen, it flicks into life revealing the most obscene image she has ever seen.

This leads to a chain of events, a series of rows, tears and recriminations that culminate with Liz filing for divorce and Tom being disciplined by his church. Then Tom gets signed off work with depression. He is still drawn to cruise the Internet for hours in the day, as well as most nights.

This story contains many elements that contribute to porn addiction. One of these is emotional and physical isolation. There are many marriages which are under strain because of the pressures of contemporary life, bringing up children, needing to pay the mortgage and so on. These stresses are not always talked through and resolved, partly because of lack of time or energy. When people become exhausted they tend to retreat into themselves and away from others. If a person already has difficulty trusting their partner or opening up emotionally to them, they may go to their own private Egypt for relief. They might seek forms of self-comforting and emotional sedation that don't depend on another human being. This may well extend to God, too. When people become very stressed and isolated they look for immediate gratification and soothing which is under their control. Unfortunately, what seems to be under their control to begin with can eventually control *them*; Egypt becomes a prison.

Another aspect of this story that is only too common is the compartmentalisation of the public persona (upstanding man in the church and community) and the private chaos of lust, and ever more desperate attempts to meet spiritual and emotional needs in all the wrong places. This is the kind of separation between a person's hidden self and public self which can result in scandals erupting in the press. These 'moral failures' can have a devastating effect not only on the individual, but also upon families and church communities. The sex addict can seem outwardly to be able to cope with more than an average person. They may be someone other people lean on. They don't complain and are actually seen as rather easy-going and unstressed. This is an entirely false persona; it is the persona of a little child who is scared to show any vulnerability or ask for help. The stress levels in such a person can be very high, driving them to seek relief in pornography. In porn they can let go and be a passive consumer of images which they have control over. They can go into a euphoric trance and forget everything else that bothers them in life. However, when they finish bingeing on porn and have to face the world again, they can be overwhelmed with remorse and shame that can in turn trigger a deeper depression.

BELIEF SYSTEM

Addicts may be so used to splitting the chaotic aspects of themselves from their public persona that there is no space in their lives to face, articulate and work through their emotional distress. This may lead to a complete lack of awareness of the consequences of their actions on themselves or others. They may be very closed off to emotion, feeling blank when they are not filled with shame and remorse. This can lead to a separation from any genuine empathy for how others are affected, or awareness of their own pain.

Carnes asserts that the sex addicts' belief system is what influences everything else. In some respects their belief system is delusional. It insulates the addict from reality. A common underlying belief is that they are worthless. Perhaps on the basis of emotional deprivation – such as the physical or emotional absence of a parent – they may believe that no one wants to, or is able to, meet their needs. This leads to a deep-rooted belief that there is therefore no hope of being known and accepted or loved. A core belief of the sex addict is 'no one would love me as I am'. They are destined to remain isolated and lonely. This leads to sex becoming their primary need, rather than relationship, because relationship is absent from their mental map. They don't trust people. They trust sex. They have a relationship with sex not people.

Because pornography doesn't involve 'real people', it can seem to the addicts' disordered thinking that they are not really affecting anyone. Chat room relationships can take the place of real ones. So people become more withdrawn from real life. If the addicts are convinced that they cannot be nurtured by other people – or God – because that fits with their developmental experience, they may turn to more individualistic ways of self-comforting. Sex can then become confused with nurture. Being secure, therefore, means to be sexual. This in turn can lead to another false belief such as 'sex is my most important need'.

SEX ADDICTION CYCLE

The sex addiction cycle follows a very similar journey to other forms of addiction.

1. Preoccupation – trance – mind engrossed with sex – intoxication – searching Internet.
2. Ritualisation – increases arousal. Habitual arrangement of area to act out in.
3. Compulsive sexual behaviour – sex act – addict cannot control or stop this.
4. Despair – possibly suicidal.

This cycle is triggered by particular experiences which resonate with the addict's areas of vulnerability. So, for example, if the addict comes from a background of feeling abandoned and disconnected from primary caregivers, being alone for any length of time can be difficult. Other triggers that can lead to the addict acting out can include a sense of needing to strive for perfection, and being entirely responsible and unable to trust other people for help. A further very common trigger for the addict can be having time on their hands that is unstructured and open-ended. This can lead to the preoccupation phase of the sex addiction cycle and from there it's a short journey to acting-out behaviour.

Life for the sex addict can – as in the example of Tom – become increasingly unmanageable. Legal consequences can arise from activities such as use of prostitutes.

ESCALATION OF ONLINE SEXUAL ADDICTION

As I said in the Introduction, pornography on the Internet has been described as the crack cocaine of sex addiction. Because of the endless variety of sexual practices available online, people can very rapidly become fixated on a level of deviancy it would have taken years to reach (if ever), before the advent of the Internet. Fantasy can escalate into action when people who contact each other online then go on to meet for sexual encounters. This can put the addict in increasingly dangerous situations.

Patrick Carnes outlines a three-stage development of arousal:

- Physical attraction
- Romance – with the euphoric release of dopamine – leading to a kind of temporary insanity
- Bonding and attachment

Neuroscience seems to show that there is an overlap between the sexual neuropathways and the neuropathways that are involved with addiction.

As an individual develops they begin to make connections or mental maps that link specific stimuli to sexual arousal. If the person is traumatised by abuse or being over-exposed to sexual stimuli these mental maps of arousal can become distorted. Exposure to pornography can be a cause as well as a consequence of these kinds of developmental changes.

Rob Bell[2] describes how lust comes from a deep lack of satisfaction with life:

> When we're not at peace, when we aren't content, when we aren't in a good place our radar gets turned on. We're looking. Searching. And we're sensory creatures so it won't be long before something, or somebody, catches our attention.

If a person is in the right place and at peace, this radar gets turned off. If they are beset by false beliefs about their worthlessness and flooded by anxiety, they may become subsumed in lustful sensations. This causes a loss of sensitivity to emotions, other people, and even the detail of the person's physical environment.

Gerald May has examined the topic of addiction from the Christian perspective. He states that humanity is supposed to desire God, to attach affections to Him. Addiction happens when affection goes elsewhere: 'Addiction is caused by the attachment or nailing, of desire to specific objects'.[3] This clinging on to objects of addiction limits the space for grace to fill a person.

ACTIVITY

The next time you decide to spend an evening watching TV or a movie, try to look at any dramatic production – including 'soaps' – in an objective way. Make a note of how much sexual content there is, overt or implied. Now think back to your teen or young adult years. On a scale of one to ten, how sexualised do you think the media has become since then? How can we avoid taking the world's attitude into our own thinking, being, and way of living?

REFLECTION
- Examine your own attitude towards 'sex addicts'. For instance, if someone admitted to you that they had a sex addiction, would you immediately assume they were giving in to lust, and had no self-control? Would you find you had more sympathy with someone caught in another addiction, such as narcotics?
- Think about the story of Tom and Liz. Who do you have more natural sympathy with?
- If you are caught in the nightmare of sex addiction yourself, think about what you have learned in this chapter, and spend some time admitting your need to Jesus – who knows, understands, loves and accepts you ... and is totally unshockable!

PRAYER
Lord Jesus, thank You that You understand how we are formed and made. You know what has led to our hurts and habits. You know why we are as we are. I invite You now to come into my situation, and bring Your light, warmth, healing and freedom. In Jesus' name. Amen.

NOTES
1   Patrick Carnes, *Out of the Shadows: Understanding Sexual Addictions* (Minnesota: Hazeldon, 2001). Much of the material in this chapter comes from this very helpful book.
2   Rob Bell, *Sex God* (Grand Rapids: Zondervan, 2007).
3   Gerald G. May, *Addiction and Grace* (New York: HarperCollins, 1991).

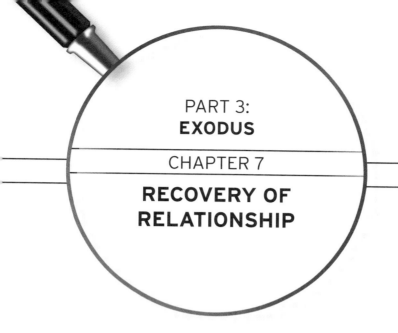

PART 3:
EXODUS

CHAPTER 7

RECOVERY OF RELATIONSHIP

We now come to look at the process of recovery from addiction. This journey towards freedom and life has some similarities with the Israelites' exodus from Egypt and the journey to the promised land. In this chapter, we will look at how this journey connects to changes in relationships.

Relationship is at the heart of the Christian understanding of God. We are created in the image of a Trinitarian God and are therefore designed to be in relationship. Healthy relating refers to three different domains: Relationship with God, relationship with the opposite sex, and relationship with others in our society. Recovery means the addict's relationships in all these spheres become freer, less fearful and more loving. This process can be slow and take time. Just as with the Israelites in the desert, learning to trust God and follow His ways rather than the familiar ways of self-sufficiency can be a tortuous process. Trust takes time to establish, particularly if an individual has been let down in the past by others.

First of all, let us look at the relational aspect of making the exodus out of the slavery of addiction.

RELATIONSHIP WITH GOD

Just as breakdown in relationships is often at the root of addictions, relationships are also at the heart of recovery.

The key relationship is that of the person with God. The Father of creation is the only one who can be relied on to heal, save and clean up the recovering addict. However, because of brokenness in relationships with earthly caregivers, it is often very difficult for people to trust God. As they look at God through the lens of their broken relationships with parents or others, their vision of God may be distorted by these past experiences. This distortion can take different forms. They may perceive God to be absent, abusive, passive, angry or simply not interested. Any one of these perceptions sets in motion a devastating chain reaction in the individual. This reaction affects belief patterns, feelings and relationships with others. So, for example, if a person believes that God is not interested in them, this may lead to a belief that they are unlovable. This in turn can trigger a turning away from God or other people as a source of love. The final part of this process is a turning to addictions that appear to act as a replacement for the absent God.

RELATIONSHIP BETWEEN THE SEXES

God created humanity as male and female. His original design for Adam and Eve was to reflect the glory of God in a complementary relationship of mutual love and respect. As a consequence of the

Fall, the beauty of this relationship has become distorted and fractured. Therefore men and women tend to perceive each other in greater or lesser degrees of distortion. In sex addiction, the addict's perception of gender and sexuality becomes broken. This brokenness has consequences in the way the addict relates to the opposite sex. So, therefore, recovery means a restoration of God-given ways of seeing the opposite gender. An example of this may be the restoration of an old painting that has become covered with grime and dirt over the years and, as the picture is cleaned up, the beauty of the original work of art is revealed in all its glory. A part of the process of this recovery of healthy relationships between the sexes will often need to include forgiveness for past hurts. Another key part of this recovery is often seen in the blessing that can occur within mixed-sex groups and friendships that are not sexualised.

RELATIONSHIPS WITHIN THE CHURCH

The Church should be a place of healing and recovery for the addict. It is in the community of the Body of Christ that they can begin to find acceptance, forgiveness, love and healing. One of the key aspects of this process is the individual's developing relationships in which they are accepted and completely known. This may be the first time that the recovering addict has not simply been known on the basis of the mask that they put forward to the world. This can be an uncomfortable and even painful process, but within safe boundaries and accountable relationships they can begin this journey. This level of honest accountability and honesty in relationships may be a challenge to some churches. However, it is essential not only for the health of the recovering addict, but for the Church as a whole that it addresses the range of human struggle. Some churches are developing systems of accountability. These can be in the form of one-to-one or group formats. In these relationships, people can bring the works of darkness out into the light and, by doing so, disempower them.

Graham Tomlin[1] has supported this view that Church communities can and should be places of recovery. However, he seems to be going further than viewing Church as a place for healing (what some have called the 'hospital model') and outlines the concept of Church as spiritual gym. Although this may sound rather prosaic, Tomlin is really calling for a rediscovery and use of the classic spiritual disciplines.

I think that engaging with disciplines such as fasting, solitude and silence is not only restorative for the recovering addict (and we will look at the issue again later in the book), but also provides a framework for prevention of possible difficulties to members of the wider Church community. Although these disciplines have often been thought of in the past as individualistic, they could also arise out of a mutually supportive framework of support and accountability in the Church. This is a model of Church as a healthy community that demonstrates God's love towards one another and the world beyond the Church. Tomlin equates learning spiritual disciplines with becoming good at a sport such as tennis. Tennis players may occasionally play good shots by accident if they don't practise. But if one trains, one hits more good shots more often! The fruit of the Spirit are not forced but flow from love. In some respects, the restoration of being able to relate well should flow from the Church into society and all parts of our culture.

ACTIVITY

Do you believe God cares about your situation? Do you believe He is even aware of it? Write a letter to Him, being honest in Your feelings. Read it back, out loud if possible, and believe He has heard. Then put the letter through a shredder. Know that God loves and accepts you, through Jesus Christ, His Son.

REFLECTION

- Do you feel God is angry and rejecting? Read John 3:16 and remember that God so loved (insert your name) that He gave His only Son. Why? So that *you* could have eternal life. Reflect on that momentous thought.
- Is there anyone in your church or circle of friends to whom you feel you could be 'accountable'? (Note: if you are helping someone caught in addiction, you might begin to pray about the need for them to have an accountability group or partner, and what this would mean in practice.)
- In what ways might your own fellowship begin to model Church as a 'spiritual gym'?

PRAYER

Loving heavenly Father, I praise You and thank You because You are interested in every detail of our lives. You made us and formed us, and redeemed us. Thank You for Your unconditional love and acceptance, in Your Son, Jesus. Thank You for that amazing love *for me* today. Amen.

NOTE

1   Graham Tomlin, *Spiritual Fitness* (London: Continuum, 2006).

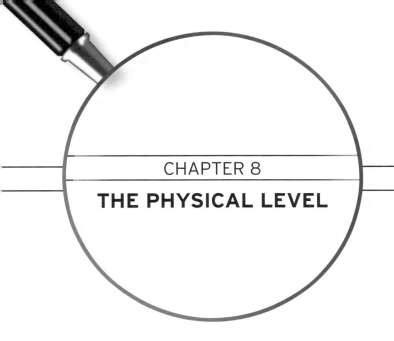

CHAPTER 8

THE PHYSICAL LEVEL

The problems which lie at the heart of addictions are as a consequence of breakdown in relationships. This relational breakdown is actually present in humanity and has always been present since the original fall of Adam and Eve from perfect relationship with God. If the problem is caused by a breakdown in relationship, then the answer is also relational, the restoring of relationship with the Father as we enter into the death, resurrection and new life of Christ. This theological truth is, however, not just abstract theory but is also intrinsic to the experience of life at a physical level. And it is at this physical and neurological level that change and recovery really brings freedom.

HEALTHY HABITS
It is important to establish healthy habits in the exodus from slavery to recovery. These habits could be described as 'repeating

patterns of action'. In the book of Exodus, we read about the Israelites' journey through the desert. Here they went through a painful process of building new habits of trust in God. The detailed creation of the tabernacle and the establishment of a liturgy around worship were instituted. The giving of the Law at Mount Sinai was a wonderful gift of God to His people that provided healthy boundaries and practices to enable them to be truly free and to enjoy the blessings of being in the family of God.

Jesus did not come to abolish the Law but to fulfil it and deepen the principles of a covenantal relationship with the Father. In doing this, He was not only leading us to make cognitive changes but, more fundamentally, He was enabling us to exchange hearts of stone for hearts of flesh (Ezek. 11:19; 36:26). This was a heart issue! This gospel is good news for the broken-hearted, the oppressed, the abandoned and imprisoned. It is a gospel of rescue for those who feel unlovable, unacceptable and outcast.

The reason this message of Christ is the answer to those caught up in addiction (not to mention everyone else – we are *all* also tainted by sin) is that the love of God is the only means by which we can be healed.

THE NEUROLOGY OF FREEDOM

The pain that causes people to build up defences that then turn into addictions is experienced physically and, therefore, at the neurological level. If a baby or child is distressed and not comforted – or, even worse, abandoned emotionally or physically – their neurological development can be affected. They have a deficiency in the chemicals that are linked to comfort and love. A baby who develops healthily will have been stroked and comforted when distressed. Scientists have said that pain can be significantly alleviated by stroking and cuddling. If this is not present, the individual will grow up with a depressed sense of wellbeing; this can form into thinking that supports and confirms their experience. This thinking is often depressed and negative.

Humans will generally seek to alleviate this kind of stress and distress. The chemical rush of addiction can suddenly flood these deprived neurological areas with the chemical dopamine which brings a euphoric high.

In an article for *The New York Times*,[1] Daniel Goleman reports that when someone takes a drug such as cocaine, it floods the neurons of the brain with levels of dopamine never seen naturally. Addictive drugs have a massive impact on the circuitry of the brain with dopamine 'storming' through the pathway with an intensity which never happens under ordinary circumstances. The systems are perturbed when drugs are taken repeatedly, and consequently try to adapt. They do this by making the dopamine less effective. This means the individual becomes dependent on the overwhelming rush of dopamine because the alternative is a depression and blunting of good feelings. So recovery must include the establishment of new habits that will reach this deep level of physical/emotional experience in the person.

In the context of Christian healing or counselling, this may mean using touch in a non-invasive and respectful way. It may include the practice of the laying on of hands. But fundamentally it is about introducing the recovering addict to the key truth that they are loved and chosen and adopted into the family of a loving Father. To some extent this is a cognitive idea, but it can move from the head to the heart given enough time, and enough work on relaxation and use of the imagination to visualise the One whose love for us is without measure. Being in relationship with people who accept and listen to the individual, whether in a recovery or church-based group, is also essential.

In those suffering from addiction it is also common for the deep part of the brain, the limbic system, to be triggered to react to stress with an impulse to run or fight, the 'fight or flight' mechanism. Addicts will find it difficult to accurately appraise a situation and the appropriate response. This is because they tend to interpret situations in fairly extreme 'all or nothing' ways. This in turn is because they have got stuck at an early stage of development where experiences and emotions which have not been soothed or regulated by caregivers become overwhelming storms of feeling. The addicts' capacity to calm themselves, keep things in perspective and regulate their own emotions is impaired. The emotional highs and lows of addiction then becomes the mechanism for managing.

This, however, makes it even more difficult to judge what's really happening. So one day when Kathy gets a call that her boss wants to talk to her, she goes into a panic, fearing that she is going to be fired. This causes her to seek out an old boyfriend and sleep with him as a way of distracting herself, and self-comforting. In fact, her boss wants to give her a pay rise! The limbic system, therefore, tends to react as if an old root pain is happening once more. This leads to catastrophic thinking, as if the original trauma is happening all over again.

It is not surprising in these circumstances that the addict seeks comfort and salvation in their drug of choice. In a sense, this is how the addict feels they can survive the catastrophic reactions arising out of old, unhealed wounds. This means that the addictive highs are not just about 'getting high', but also to manage high levels of stress.

REVIEWING THE CYCLE

So let's return to the addiction cycle again, and think of different ways of handling each of the different stages.

The first stage was the red flags – when the stress levels start going up. There will be particular situations that trigger people. Here it's all about self-awareness, where we encourage a person to think back over their particular history, remember the times when they have done whatever their addiction is, and to *slow everything down*.

It's sometimes helpful to think about the last episode. For example, a shopaholic might say: 'I went into a shop and bought everything in sight. I don't know how long I was in there for, and I don't even remember how I got in or how I got out, but I do know that when I came home I had boxes and boxes of clothes I didn't want. I just wanted to throw them all away.'

Here, we really want to get back to what happened *just before* that whole episode started – the red flag. It is really important that the addicted person begins to list the particular things that are likely to act as a trigger for them; if they don't, they are not going to be able to avoid them or deal with them in any other way. So for the shopaholic it might be that they were stressed because somebody had criticised them – they might have low self-esteem, so if they get criticised they might have a tendency to go off and comfort themselves by shopping. By realising this, the person should become more aware that they need to be careful how they react when they feel criticised. The key thing is always to slow everything down, to breathe more deeply and to not just react on the spur of the moment.

We are not looking for the people to deny the patterns that they get into – often people are ashamed – but it's better if they

73

can identify them. And the 'halt' acrostic is quite helpful, which is to ask:

Are you:
Hungry,
Alone,
Lonely or
Tired?

These are often triggers – or red flags – for people. So somebody might do something addictive when they are tired, or they have had a long day, or they have just come home and they are hungry and they are on their own. That can be a dangerous time.

What we have been looking at here is changing reflexes. Once these things have been identified, as well as slowing everything down and breathing more deeply, the person needs to be helped to focus on reality. It's quite amazing, actually, that when addicted people go back over these episodes they can find that everything has got blanked out except the thing they are focusing on; we can see here the whole issue of desire being focused on the addiction rather than on God. It also blanks out everything else around it, so if we are trying to help someone in an addiction, we would encourage the person, when they start going into their cycle, to slow down and maybe look around them to see what's in the room, notice who's around, what the time is, and just to try and stay in reality; if they are a Christian, we would suggest they start praying at that point, asking God to come into that moment and hold them and give them the security they need.

Remember, it's slowing everything down and avoiding the instant reflex!

In terms of the ritual, it's simply common sense – it's not going to those places, the shopaholic not going to the shopping mall; it's like the saying, 'If you don't want to get to the destination, don't get on the train!' Once someone is on the train, the chances are that they are going to go to the destination. So once the shopaholic is in the car, and then at the shopping mall, then inside a shop, it is going to be 100 times more difficult to stop than right at the beginning when they realise they are struggling. So it's really about not going to the usual places, not doing the usual things, or meeting the usual people. It's just changing the ritual.

People may find it very helpful to plan what are sometimes called 'escape strategies' before any of this even starts. An escape strategy works like this: once a person has identified their own personal stress times – perhaps when they are alone or tired – then, before the next time, they might plan: 'What will I do to get out of that moment?' There are usually different options. One might be to phone someone who is an accountability partner, somebody who knows what the addict is struggling with and who will talk and pray at short notice. Another option could be to do something physical; to go out for a walk or do something else pleasurable – go to the cinema, for instance – but to actually have planned this, to have written these things down, before the situation starts. And what the person needs to do is to practise those things when they are feeling OK, well before things get out of hand. In effect, to have a dry run!

And finally in terms of release and consequences – if the person stops doing their addiction they may actually feel more suffering. They may feel more anxiety, in the short term anyway. Leanne Payne[2] talks about this quite a bit. The idea of staying at the foot of the cross and suffering at the cross is a powerful one:

just staying there in the pain, staying with it at the feet of Jesus, and bringing it up and into the cross and into Jesus. That's where visualisation and the imagination are really helpful, because there may not always be another person there to help. Therefore, to almost train people to stay at the cross and do that when they feel pain is very, very helpful for them. And the ultimate consequence is that instead of shame and fear and guilt, there is new life, peace and freedom.

THE PATHWAY TO RECOVERY

There are some key marks of a person's successful recovery. These are:

- The ability to accept one's limitations. For some people this means giving up trying to be God and surrendering their will to Him.
- A letting go of resentment and complaining. Resentment is one of the most toxic emotions for a recovering addict. It is best replaced by establishing habits of thanksgiving, praise, worship and gratitude.
- A surrendering of one's life to God or a higher power. This is a state of mind that requires continual working on, rather than just a single act.

Recovery groups such as AA have short phrases that are often helpful for people working towards recovery. These phrases summarise core principles of the ideas listed above.

- Live and let live!
- Let go and let God.

- Easy does it!
- One day at a time.

So, addicts, when they feel themselves slipping back into what is habitual for them, should learn to stop at the moment of decision. If addicts just decide to not do what they think they should do *because it feels so familiar*, then their true and natural way of being will spring up without them even having to think about it

It's not a struggle to 'do it right' – that's the Law, and it makes us behave in unnatural and inhuman ways. It is trusting that if we don't do our usual – and what feels like normal – addictive reaction, we will find another way … and that the other way is already there. In essence, we are truly entering into our 'homeland', our natural way of being – the way God has made us to be. Our promised land, if you like!

ACTIVITY

Look at the four phrases above – Live and let live; Let go and let God; Easy does it; One day at a time. Be creative; write them down on a piece of card, frame and hang on a wall; design a bookmark and keep in your Bible or by your bed; or use them as a screensaver.

REFLECTION

- Think about times when you are vulnerable. Is it when you are **H**ungry, **A**lone, **L**onely or **T**ired? What strategies can you put in place so that you can learn to stop at the moment of decision?
- Reflect on what it means to be thankful, grateful, and in an attitude of surrender to God in your daily life. If you could live

like this every day, how might your inner life change?

• Think about your natural 'homeland'. What do you think it looks like?

PRAYER

Lord God, I thank and praise You for all You are teaching me. Lord, help me to stay humble, be full of gratitude and content in the life You have chosen for me. Today I surrender to Your goodness and grace. Amen.

NOTES

1   Daniel Goleman, 'Brain Images of Addiction', *The New York Times*, 13 August 1996.

2   Leanne Payne, *Restoring the Christian Soul* (Eastbourne: Kingsway, 1994).

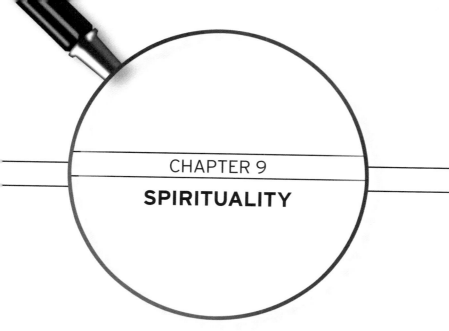

CHAPTER 9

SPIRITUALITY

People become addicted because they are trying to avoid pain. It's important that they invite Jesus into that pain; to actually come and be with them in it. This is different from them having to hold it all themselves – in essence, looking at Jesus at a distance, looking at them. They are inviting Jesus to come and stand with them, and be with them and in them in that pain.

I was seeing somebody once who, as they were going through their pain, actually felt the arms of God around them – so tangible that they thought *I* was actually holding them. But it wasn't me, it was God.

Some people, perhaps because of their upbringing, have never had the experience of being held and contained; this is something primarily parents are meant to give. I think sometimes God is more than able to physically hold people, and certainly to give them that strong sense of His presence around them, enveloping them and containing their painful feelings. When God does this, it is a profound healing experience that can relieve stress to a great degree, and the addictions that come from it. So, we must always remember to pray the Lord into the addict's experience of pain.

PLEASURE IN GOD

Another key issue – one which might be a bit surprising, and one that Christians often overlook, but which I think is crucial – is the issue of pleasure; taking pleasure in God.

There is a version of Christianity that is pretty popular even now, which is a little averse to the idea of taking pleasure in God. This kind of Christianity believes that faith is to do with the mind, and understanding God, and working God out. But it seems fairly clear that God does enjoy our company and wants *relationship* with us. If He has given His Son to suffer and die on our behalf so that He can have relationship with us, it seems that relationship is highly important to God and that He takes great pleasure in us.

Because addiction is so much a feeling- and pleasure-based thing, it seems to make sense that if we are to help people to break free from addiction then it's really important to introduce them to the God who loves them in a passionate sense – not just in their minds, but emotionally as well.

PASSIONATE GOD

If addiction is caused by desire gone awry or desire bent towards the created rather than the Creator, then the solution is to enter into a passionate, emotional relationship with God in the Spirit and through Jesus. I certainly think the Trinity is characterised by joyful love. 1 Thessalonians 4:3–5 talks about people who are living in abandon to their own sin and sensuality, and at the end of verse 5 we read that they are doing this because they 'do not know God'. In that sense, 'know' is to know in a very deep, intimate way. I think that once we come to know God like this, and once we enable people to know God in this way – not just by cerebral head knowledge, but in a heart-based, emotional, strongly passionate, intimate kind of way – then this actually begins to blot out all of the other stuff that seemed so enticing and so exciting about addiction. How are we ever going to help people to come out of powerful addictions which give them huge highs, when we offer a God who is drained of emotion and passion? That seems to be short-changing them at best! This is a key issue for addictions.

Rob Bell[1] argues that desire, far from being repressed, should be attached to God. Love for God can consume a person with holy desire: 'It's not about getting rid of desire. It's about giving ourselves to bigger and better and more powerful desires'. So, recovery is not all about giving something up, it's about redirecting our life energy towards something more beautiful. As Bell says, 'How can you make your life about *that* so you won't be tempted to give in to *this*?'

Gerald May[2] advocates detachment which 'aims at correcting one's own anxious grasping in order to free oneself for committed relationship with God'. Detachment frees our desire to pursue God. May describes this as freedom!

Psalm 37:4 states, 'Delight yourself in the LORD and he will give you the desires of your heart.' What does it mean, to delight in the Lord? This is a transferring of our affections, love and attachments from the dead objects onto which we have clung and into the living One with whom we can have relationship. It is to draw up the waters of life from the wells of salvation (see Isa. 12:3). When the Israelites were on the borders of the promised land, they tasted of the firstfruits. This was a sign of being fed and delighted by the provision of God.

ACTIVITY

Be still and try to imagine God's arms around you. How do you think it would feel, to be hugged by God? What effect might it have on your feelings of love, warmth and security?

REFLECTION

- God loves you in a passionate sense – not just in your mind, but emotionally as well. Spend some time meditating on that fact.
- Is *your* God drained of emotion and passion? Why not ask Him to reveal Himself to you as the God who longs for intimate relationship with His people.
- What would it mean for you to delight yourself in the Lord?

PRAYER

Loving heavenly Father, I thank You that You so desire an emotional relationship with me, Your child. I really want to know You, Lord, to hear Your voice and to follow You. I want to love You with all my heart, as well as all my mind. I invite You into my situation (or into the situation of someone you are helping) and thank You, Jesus, that You care so much. Amen.

NOTES
1   Rob Bell, *Sex God* (Grand Rapids: Zondervan 2007), p.73.
2   Gerald G. May, *Addiction and Grace* (New York: HarperCollins, 1991).

PART 4:
OCCUPYING THE LAND

CHAPTER 10

BEGINNING TO LIVE NEW STORIES

The love of Christ not only sets us free from past addictions, but we also become free to live the kingdom life. In a sense, we begin to occupy the land that God has bought for us – our promised land of recovery – and begin to live new stories.

SPIRITUAL DISCIPLINES

It's so important that we don't just focus on helping people to be delivered of addiction, because that is really only half the battle! The other half is helping people to live out their lives in a different way, a way that will lead them *towards life* rather than towards death. This is really another subject that we cannot cover here, but the starting point must be in thinking about spiritual disciplines, something we touched on earlier – especially solitude and silence.

SOLITUDE AND SILENCE

The key spiritual discipline that people with addictions find extremely difficult is solitude and silence. If you talk to anybody in the grip of an addiction, they don't know the meaning of the words 'solitude and silence' because that's the one thing they would avoid! This is because it is in solitude and silence that the true self comes up to meet the God of the real, and it's quite a painful thing. However, it is also a very healing thing.

Right from the word 'go' in our attempts to help people with addictions, we are trying to slow the process down, hoping to help them to come back to themselves – come back to how they really feel, experience how they feel, own it, confess it, talk about it, bring it to God, invite God into it and sit with God quietly in their own hearts.

It's not about rushing onto the next distraction, the next buzz, the next high, the next thing that's going to make it right for them. Part of this freedom is to face an experience of what is really being felt – we must remember that addicts are very expert at medicating away all their feelings.

TALK ABOUT IT!

The next part of the process is to experience and talk about these feelings with trusted friends or people who might be described as 'accountability partners'. This is why being in small groups or even in prayer triplets or accountability groups is so important; it actually enables the person who is coming out of this very lonely, isolated, shameful world of addiction to discover the freedom and acceptance that the Church, the Body of Christ, can offer as a place of healthy relationship, of openness, of things not being hidden in darkness but brought into the light. So the Church in the form of small groups becomes a big part of people's onward journey, as they move out of addiction.

STEPS TO RECOVERY

It is very helpful when looking at the process of recovery from addiction, to think about the programme which has been put together by Alcoholics Anonymous. The programme was originally constructed by evangelical Christians, and although these days most would probably talk about relying on a 'higher power', originally that would have been God – and we can still take it to mean God. Here, I will just talk about the first three steps because these are the key steps for somebody beginning to break free of their addiction.

STEP 1

The first step is the person admitting that they are powerless over their addiction, and that their life has become unmanageable. The purpose of this step is to help the person to give up the illusion of being in control. This denotes a fundamental choice to turn from doing things the way the addict has previously chosen. To change the direction of one's life in this way could be described as repentance. To repent is to turn away from the insanity of self-sufficiency and independence and turn towards a life of surrender to God. To repent is to recognise that one's own sinful attempts at self-comfort are bankrupt. It is to recognise that the devastating stain of addiction will not be eradicated by human effort. It is to accept that only God has provided the means by which light can shine into the darkness of addiction. The sacrificial death of Christ to restore relationship with the Father is in complete contradiction of addicts' belief that they have to be the god of their own lives.

Usually addictions are fuelled and driven by some kind of illusion; the person feels that they are in control of their problems and, if they just try a bit harder, if they just get the magic formula right, they will be able to fix everything. It's like the person who gets drunk every Friday, saying on Saturday, 'I'll never do it again!' – they *know* it's the last time they will ever do it! Step 1 is really about encouraging the person to come to the point of admitting that their best efforts have got them where they are now. A phrase often used in recovery groups is 'my best efforts, my best thinking, the best of the best of what I could come up with is what's got me here' and this is the best starting point – give up that sense of control and admit a sort of powerlessness!

STEP 2
Step 2 is coming to believe that a power greater than oneself can restore sanity – that God can restore sanity to the person, and that they are going to be totally reliant on Him to do that.

You can see that these steps are, in reality, 'all or nothing'. It entirely depends on the person handing their life over to God, depending on Him to help them, and giving up all control over their lives – because their own best efforts to 'control' their lives have driven them into the state they are in.

STEP 3
The third step is to make a decision to turn one's will over – one's life over – to the care of God. This can be a controversial idea because we often think that we need to exercise our will. But from a Christian perspective, our wills can be so damaged, so broken by sin and by our addiction that we need to turn that over

to God along with the rest of us. We need to 'turn ourselves in', and let Him repair the damage and bring us to a point where we can start to find freedom and healing.

ENOUGH NOW!

It is perhaps worth saying again at this point that addiction is a response to feelings of deprivation and need. So the recovering addict needs to learn that they can come to God, saying, 'Give me more.' People often have an orphan/pauper mentality, going around in psychological rags. However, the issue is to have a spirit of wisdom and revelation as to what they already have in Christ: they have enough *now*. The issue for the addict is being able to ask for it and to take it in – to draw up water from the wells of salvation; to eat and drink of His body and blood.

ACTIVITY

'… in our attempts to help people with addictions, we are trying to slow the process down, hoping to help them … come back to how they really feel, experience how they feel, own it, confess it, talk about it, bring it to God, invite God into it and sit with God quietly in their own hearts.' Can you sit quietly with God, and invite Him into your situation today?

REFLECTION

- Look at the steps above. How helpful might they be in your own life, or in the life of the person you are helping?
- If you struggle to turn your will over to God, ask yourself why. It might help to discuss your findings with a trusted Christian counsellor or friend.

- Are you in rags, or can you ask your heavenly Father, 'Give me more?' If you can't quite do that, ask Him to give you the power to live and move in all that He has for you.

PRAYER

Lord Jesus Christ, Son of the living God, I praise and worship You for all that You are and all that You have done for me. Help me to live totally in Your freedom, the freedom You bought for me on the cross. Help me to live free, Jesus, in every aspect of my being, as I begin to live my new story. In Your wonderful name I ask it. Amen.

CHAPTER 11

NEW STORIES FOR OLD

At the heart of the Christian faith is a story, a narrative. Story is deeply human. If you ask a person to describe or define themselves they will answer you with a story – a story about who they are. Our lives are shaped by the stories we tell ourselves, and the stories others tell about us. We live, move and have our being in story. This is why stories are so important to children; they explain their world, they provide shape and structure with which to make sense of life.

FALSE REALITIES

The story at the heart of Christianity is one of deliverance from captivity. N.T. Wright[1] has pointed to strong echoes between the Exodus of the Israelites from slavery in the Old Testament, and the work of Christ in freeing those held captive, as announced in Luke 4:18.

I believe that at the core of any addiction is a person held captive by a lie, a false attachment that offers freedom and delivers a slow death. Addicts are often unaware of the captivity they are in. Moreover, the addiction acts as their god. It defines who they are and shapes their existence. Walter Brueggemann[2] has written persuasively about the way in which God's people have often become entranced by the culture that holds them captive – for example, in the Babylonian Exile.

A key part of this narrative of enslavement is that the truth of who they are is lost, and a false set of 'truths' dominate their thinking, feeling and behaviour. This false reality will surface in the belief system of the person, particularly in the context of identity. So assumptions will be made that 'I am ...' which are usually quite self-limiting, or even filled with despair and self-hatred; for example, 'I am on my own; no one can help me, I am beyond help.' This can lead to a perpetual state of despair – what in previous times has been described as a spirit of *acedia*, or sloth, a giving up on life. This can be masked by a manic defence of 'live fast, die young' or a perpetual cynicism about life that can also manifest as depression. Addiction is often linked to this kind of existential despair.

In the field of narrative therapy, there is a strong awareness of these 'problem saturated stories'. Michael White[3] in particular describes how these stories shape and control not only individuals but whole families.

CHANGE

So, how does the story of captivity to addiction and death (or in biblical language, idolatry) change to a story of freedom and life? The short answer is 'the gospel' – it's Jesus entering into our experience, the depths of our emptiness and shame; He brings an exodus from slavery and ushers us into the promised land of relationship with God and each other.

Although this theme of rescue, deliverance and freedom is at the heart of the Bible, I want to focus on one particular story from the Gospel of John that I believe highlights this change in narrative very effectively. That is, Jesus' meeting with the woman at the well (John 4). The transition from slavery/addiction to freedom has three components, and these are well illustrated in this story. In Jesus' meeting with the Samaritan woman, we can see

1. The old story of captivity and slavery – addiction.
2. The new story of God's love, freedom and grace.
3. The dialogue between these two stories – the journey from captivity to freedom.

This process can also be viewed as similar to what has been described as the 'liminal stages'. These are the transitions often undertaken in rites of passage. The person starts with living out the story of their lives as they know it. They then move into a period of transition that is marked by confusion. The final stage is of coming into a new – and probably more expansive – narrative that changes identity. This rite of passage journey seems to fit with key narratives such as the Exodus.

TRANSFORMATION

Let us now attempt to unpack the way that old narratives can be transformed at the meeting point between our account, or story, of our lives and God's. This is, of course, a general theological motif, but one which I think is particularly relevant to those imprisoned in addictions. (At this point, I would recommend reading *The Shack*[4] as this book provides a very helpful narrative that shows how transformative this kind of dialogue between God and us can be.) So let's turn to the woman at the well, contrasting the addict's narrative with God's, and the resulting new narrative.

Addict's narrative

- Verse 9. The woman makes a distinction between herself and Jesus. She is a Samaritan, He is a Jew and the two are not meant to have any dealings with each other. This is just the first of several statements about who she is. It immediately limits her contact with Jesus (or so she thinks). There may also be a hint of inferiority and self-condemnation implicit in her statement.
- Like most addicts (and, in fact, most people in general) the woman clings onto her interpretation of reality. She thinks she knows all about this well and points out to Jesus that it is deep and He has nothing to draw water with (v.11). She has a whole story to back up her perception that goes all the way back to Jacob. This is rather similar to Brueggemann's[5] idea of restating the official story. I also see this as similar to Elijah, in 1 Kings 19, telling God repeatedly how hopeless his situation is! Addicts in particular have a very inflated perspective of how big their problems are. They tend to believe that God is smaller than their problems, and that therefore they have to take matters into their own hands and find their own solutions. It is almost comical that when Jesus arrives offering another source of water that the woman assumes *He* is mistaken and tries to educate Him as to *how things really are*!
- In verse 20, the woman says, in effect, 'Our fathers have always

worshipped on *this* mountain. This is how we have always done it. No one ever questions our long-standing attachment to this thing!' Many addicts would never question why they are attached to the object of their addiction.

God's narrative

- Verse 10: 'If you knew …' Although from a God perspective, the woman's limited view of reality is clear, there seems to be understanding and compassion for her limitations. Her limitations are not judged.
- '… the gift …' Addicts think *they* have to make everything happen. They have to save themselves. They are not aware of the love and grace that comes to them as a free gift. For addicts, love and acceptance are always conditional on them earning it.
- '… you would [ask]' The addict has to reach out beyond their despair and hopelessness to receive what they really need. This requires hope and vision that there is something more, something out there to reach out for.
- '… living water.' This is a familiar symbol – water. The woman has been drawing up water, but it is a dead and dim echo of the living reality that Christ refers to here. Living water is not stagnant; it moves, it's relational and it dances between and through people.
- '… he would [give] you'. Healing comes from the otherness of Christ; not as in the person-centred approach – that healing comes from within. It's receiving from the other.
- A key element in this healing narrative is God's hospitality towards what the woman probably judges as non-acceptable in her life. A characteristic of addicts is self-hatred and self-condemnation.

This is far from Christ's acceptance. What we detach from and cut off from in ourselves, Christ embraces – most profoundly at the cross, where He takes it all into His body.

- Verse 13: 'Everyone who drinks this water will be thirsty again'. Human solutions are not solutions!
- Verse 14: '... whoever *drinks* the water *I* give ...' (my italics). The addict has to reach out and take otherness into themselves, emotionally, spiritually and physically. There may be overtones of communion here. And I believe that this feast is potentially a key sacrament in the healing of addicts.
- '... the water I give ... will become ... a spring of water welling up to eternal life' or another translation, 'shall be in him a well of water springing up into everlasting life' (AV).
- In verses 21–24, Jesus introduces the theme of worship of the Father. This dance of worship is not to be confined to human rules and tradition or place. This is about spirit, and our best efforts won't get us there. This is Jesus, our rescuer from dead wells!

The new dialogue leading to a new narrative

- Verse 11. Questions open up new horizons and new possibilities. The woman starts to glimpse there is another way, another solution to her addictive thirst: 'Where can you get this living water?'
- Then there is the reaching out to receive the new water in verse 15: '... give me this water'.
- In verses 17–18 the old story of failure (several husbands) is touched and revealed before the new story can be told. The pain and damage of people's lives being brought into the light is an important part of the healing process, and these verses may serve to emphasise this fact. This process is very evident

in recovery group programmes, as well as in what the Church would describe as 'confession and repentance'.

- Verses 39–42: The woman immediately comes out of her social isolation, out of her prison of shame, and re-engages with her community.

Instead of drawing up our own water, we are given new, living water by Christ; we need relationship with Him. As a result of this relationship, the individual's relationship with themselves changes.

A key element in this story is that of worship. Worship lifts the individual above their circumstances and helps them engage with otherness. Addicts stay in a room of their own making and don't realise that the world outside is changing. That's why they can have a 'Peter Pan' quality about them. Coming out of addiction is like coming out of a dream!

ACTIVITY
Put on a Christian CD or worship tape, and spend some time worshipping God.

REFLECTION
- Think about what it means to trade 'old' for 'new.' Reflect on your own feelings when you have perhaps bought a new piece of furniture, a new car … How wonderful to know that we can trade our old ways of living for new! Praise God for His goodness.
- Think about some of your 'old narratives'. How might they be changed by an encounter with God's love, freedom and grace?
- Look again at the story of Jesus' encounter with the woman in John 4. Read it slowly in the light of what you have learned, and

be aware of the transformation taking place. If it helps, imagine you are either that woman, or that you are at the well and Jesus has a similar conversation with you. Try to visualise the heat of the day, the isolation of the moment. What does Jesus say to you? And how do you respond?

PRAYER

Lord Jesus, thank You that You are more than willing to meet us in our addictions, that You offer peace, acceptance, freedom and life in abundance. Thank You for Your Spirit, welling up inside us to eternal life. What an amazing gift; what an amazing God. Thank You, Jesus, that You can make all things new, for You are the God of the second chance. Amen.

NOTES

1   N.T. Wright, *The New Testament and the People of God* (London: SPCK, 1992).

2   Walter Brueggemann, *Hopeful Imagination* (Philadelphia: Fortress Press, 1986).

3   Michael White and David Epston, *Narrative Means to Therapeutic Ends* (New York: W.W. Norton, 1990).

4   William P. Young, *The Shack* (London: Hodder & Stoughton, 2008).

5   Walter Brueggemann, op. cit.

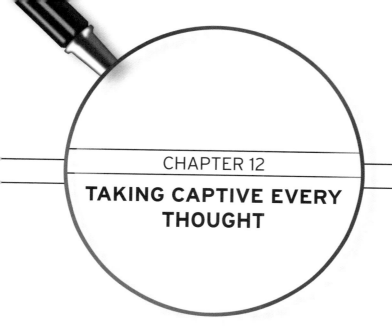

CHAPTER 12

TAKING CAPTIVE EVERY THOUGHT

When the Israelites did finally return to the land promised to them by God, they took decisions that had far-reaching and long-standing consequences for the people of God. They did not fully occupy the land.

Perhaps some of the fear of their enemies resurfaced, or perhaps they were so content with what they had that they did not see the need to follow God's instruction to subdue and rule over the land of promise. However, God's promises need to be grasped and held onto until they reach full fruition. The Israelites did build up a powerful and, at times, prosperous kingdom. But their failure to root out their enemies – and the worship of other gods – meant that they had frequent struggles with the forces that sought their destruction.

It is important in the recovery of addicts that they do not find themselves in the half-and-half situation of having a degree of sobriety but still living out of old thought patterns – 'For as [a man] thinketh in his heart, so is he' (Prov. 23:7, AV). The old patterns of thought are almost certainly key drivers in the establishment and maintenance of addictions. These thought patterns themselves often arise out of painful experiences, such as rejection or abandonment or abuse. These patterns of thought usually contain fixed beliefs such as 'I am unlovable', 'I cannot trust anyone' or 'I am on my own'. Thoughts like this do not come from nowhere. They are usually the result of coming to a fixed conclusion about oneself after being hurt. If these thought patterns are set at a young age they can become strongholds of belief that affects the individual's sense of who they are. In the case of many living addicted lives, there is even an absence of any sense of having a self. Some have described this phenomenon as a loss of a sense of being.[1] This means a lack of a solid or stable sense of selfhood.

ORPHAN OR ADOPTED CHILD

For a person with these established thought patterns, they are convinced that they know they are indeed worthless, rejected and unlovable. It is therefore difficult for the recovering addict to accept that they can trust anything or anyone other than their addiction.

It can be particularly difficult for those being counselled in a Christian context to grasp the concept of God as a loving Father. Their view of father or parent may be shaped and distorted by their early life experiences. These can cause the person to view God through the lens of fear, rejection and disappointment.

Mark Stibbe[2] has written about the 'orphan' ways of thinking as contrasted with the adoptive son paradigm. Romans 8:15–17 describes the difference between the spirit that leads to fear and the adoption into God's family that leads to freedom. In one sense this is similar to the living out of a new story as discussed earlier; indeed, as the recovering addict begins to identify their 'orphan' ways of thinking and chooses to turn towards 'adoptive' thinking, their lived-out lives are changed. An example may be that of Frances.

> Frances had long believed that her mother preferred her sister, Angela, to her. Frances was an unplanned child, over eight years younger than her sister. One day, she noticed her mother talking to Angela. Frances had been free from her gambling addiction for a couple of months now but she still felt the old temptation to assume her mother and sister were talking critically about her. At this point, she could adopt the very familiar (and therefore easier) response of feeling pushed out, judged and rejected – or choose the more unfamiliar response of thanking God for being a loved, chosen and adopted child of the Father.

The signs of an 'orphan tendency' are beliefs and feelings that revolve around being rejected, criticised, and often a nameless dread of being punished. These kinds of thought patterns can lead addicts, or potential addicts, to feel swamped by anxiety and restlessness. They may often take on an anti-authority or rebellious stance in relation to any authority figure. The addiction itself can be a form of rebellion against feared figures of authority. The problem with this response is that the person may rebel against authority and then find themselves emotionally alone. There is often a sense with people struggling with addiction that they do not believe anyone else can be trusted to help them, or even *wants* to help them. Therefore they have to take matters into their own hands and do everything themselves.

This approach has two immediate consequences. First, they feel exhausted and defeated. This especially happens if they are trying to gain acceptance and approval from others by performance – by getting Daddy's approval by being better than the rest. Many high-achieving addicts are constantly driven into overwork and stress by their orphan hearts that long for approval from someone who will just say, 'Well done.'

The second consequence of this response is that apart from getting tired and stressed, the person is also taking on responsibility for controlling the whole of their lives – and they are simply not equipped or meant to take this on. This is a task that can only be entrusted to a heavenly Father. Although this is a Christian response, AA, Gamblers Anonymous and Sex Addicts Anonymous have as their second step the statement that 'we have come to believe that we can only trust in a power higher than ourselves', as we saw earlier.

More subtle aspects of these orphan thought patterns can be an ironic or sarcastic sense of humour which masks a sense of sloth or *acedia*, again as I mentioned before. Sloth is one of the 'deadly sins' and relates to a giving up on God's goodness. It is rooted in despair and hopelessness. There is a heavy sense that nothing really matters. The individual in this state has no sense of accepting themselves and, in fact, probably has a deep hatred for all aspects of themselves. The emotional orphan has had to build up walls and defences to protect them from further hurt or abandonment. They have long since stopped waiting to be looked after, cared for or cherished. Those who have been sexually abused may be particularly fearful of love or affection.

WHAT DOES IT MEAN?

So what does it mean to 'take captive every thought' (2 Cor. 10:5)? To not allow these strongholds of negative thinking to re-establish patterns of addiction! To begin with, it is important for the sufferer to identify that they have orphan patterns of thought. As we have seen, these may lie beneath tendencies such as striving to be noticed or approved of. More fundamentally, there will be core beliefs about being unacceptable or unlovable. There will probably be a tendency to rebel against authority, as well as a deep tiredness brought on by trying to control the universe alone.

It is probably advisable to work on these thought patterns when the addict is in a period of sobriety, as they will be able to address their thinking more clearly. When people are 'using' they are temporarily out of their minds and this kind of self-reflection and raising of awareness is all but impossible.

Once they are able to clarify these belief systems, the addict will have a greater opportunity of choosing alternative responses. In Christian counselling, this person can be encouraged to meditate on the heavenly Father who created them. This will initially bring up resistance and tension in the body as the old fears, and even anger, surface. The person at this point can be encouraged to look at Father God, or into the eyes of Jesus. This is a safe focus – although it may initially be very difficult to do.

THE IMAGINATION

I have mentioned before the importance of visualisation and imagination. It is vital in the healing of the orphan belief patterns that underpin addictions to engage the imagination.

I do not believe that the passions and neurological storms of addiction can simply be wished away by forcing new ways of thinking; I believe that these changes need to be rooted in the body, the place where the addictive reactions are felt.

One of the means by which mind and body communicate with each other is via the right brain. The right hemisphere of the brain is responsible for artistic impulses, creativity and emotional experiences. This is the aspect of the mind that perhaps equates most with the 'heart' in Hebrew thought; the seat of imagination and emotional responses. So this is the part of the mind that can be accessed with true and healthy images and pictures about self.

It is important in any therapeutic or healing process that the body is as much at rest as possible. Addicts are usually very out of touch with their bodies and therefore are probably also unaware of their emotions. Emotions are felt in the body, so getting in touch with the body is essential if the person is to access their emotions. Why is it important to access emotions? Because the addict is so used to masking and sedating their pain with artificially produced highs that they have come to either fear their feelings, lose all awareness of having any feelings, or both.

So it's important for the person in recovery to start looking after their physical body by having periods of rest. It is useful here to employ relaxation strategies to help enter into prayer. Another useful tool that spiritual disciplines such as the Ignatian tradition provide is the use of imagination exercises. Here the person may take an image or narrative from the Bible and place themselves in that picture. Stories such as the Lost Son (Luke 15:11–32) can be very helpful for those working on coming out of the orphan mindset. Relaxation and this kind of focused meditation on image or narrative can help the person reshape their ways of thinking. This in turn provides a more secure base from which to tackle the ups and downs of life without recourse to their drug of choice.

A NOTE TO COUNSELLORS

I have not mentioned counselling much in this book. That is partly because I am assuming those with a general interest in addiction may not necessarily be involved with counselling. As I have also indicated, the most common treatment for addiction is in a group format such as AA. However, if the sufferer is in counselling, all the orphan tendencies mentioned above are likely to arise. It is important that the therapist maintains a consistent position of respect and affirmation toward the client as they will surely be encouraged to reject them, just as they feel so many have done before. The counselling relationship may be the first time the addicted person has been with someone who does not punish or reject them when they make mistakes or slip up. Whether the addict is relating to a counsellor, a friend, a group or God they will begin to make breakthroughs when they start to let go of the need to control everything, and begin to rest and trust in another. As we have already seen, AA have clearly identified that surrendering to a higher power is essential to recovery. I think that Colossians 1:17 is a key verse in this respect – all things hold together in Christ. This must mean that addicts themselves (as all of us) can be held together not by their own efforts but by the One through whom they were created. 'It does not … depend on man's desire or effort, but on God's mercy' (Rom. 9:16). At the cross, Christ entered fully into the human experience of emptiness, pain, rejection and emptiness and took this into His body. This physical identification with the human physical/emotional state provides a means by which the addict can know they are loved and brought back into a relationship with the Father.

In Romans 8 we read 'if the Spirit of him who raised Jesus from the dead is living in you, he who raised Christ from the dead will also give life to your mortal bodies through his Spirit, who lives in you' (v.11). This is the ultimate hope for the addict who is taking the journey out of slavery and captivity to the promised land of restored relationship with God, others and self.

FREEDOM
Galatians 5:1–18 makes a contrast between freedom and the restrictions and compulsions of the flesh. Marks of the non-addict are:

- Integration with one's body
- Flexibility
- Focus – a purpose in life
- Balance of knowing truth and living it out
- Risk-taking
- Self-acceptance

We are supposed to be like trees. Wild and fully ourselves but cultivated and pruned by God, not choked by vines and ivy! This is true freedom, not independence and rebellion followed by the empty maelstrom of feelings with no boundaries!

ACTIVITY
Do you find it hard to think of God as a loving Father? Read the story of the Lost Son in Luke 15:11–32. Look at the father's response to his child – unconditional love and lavish acceptance! This is a wonderful example of the fatherhood of God. *This* is what God the Father feels towards you, His child.

REFLECTION

- In Romans 8 we read 'if the Spirit of him who raised Jesus from the dead is living in you, he who raised Christ from the dead will also give life to your mortal bodies through his Spirit, who lives in you' (v.11). Remember that this is your ultimate hope as you take the journey out of slavery and captivity to the promised land of restored relationship with God, others and self. If it helps, write the verse down on Post-it notes and stick them in places you will often see them – the kitchen, your desk, the bathroom!
- What have you gained from this Insight book? Imagine Jesus sitting in a chair beside you. Talk to Him about it, and imagine Him listening to you. What might He be saying?
- If you are in the process of counselling someone in the grip of an addiction, spend some time reflecting on material from this book that has really spoken to you, and how this might help the person you are counselling. You might like to spend some time in prayer for the person.

PRAYER

Father God, please give me Your strength, Your peace, and a sense of Your presence on my continuing journey out of Egypt into my promised land. Father, You were with the Israelites as they came out of Egypt and travelled in the wilderness. Be my pillar of cloud during the day, and my pillar of fire at night. You promise never to leave me or forsake me, and for this I praise You. Come by Your Spirit and fill me anew today, for Your power is made perfect in weakness. Amen.

NOTES

1   L. Payne, *Restoring the Christian Soul* (Eastbourne: Kingsway, 1994).
2   Mark Stibbe, *From Orphans to Heirs: Celebrating Our Spiritual Adoption* (Oxford: Bible Reading Fellowship, 1999).

SOME USEFUL CONTACTS

For alcoholism:
www.alcoholics-anonymous.org.uk
National helpline: 0845769 7555

For family and friends of alcoholics:
www.al-anonuk.org.uk
Also based on the Twelve Steps and Twelve Traditions adapted from AA:

For sexual addiction:
www.saa-recovery.org
www.living-waters-uk.org
Helpline: 020 7630 1044

For gambling addiction:
www.gamblersanonymous.org.uk

To help fight Internet temptation:
www.covenanteyes.com
Offers Internet accountability and Internet filtering.

A book we can recommend on accountability groups for men is *Samson and the Pirate Monks* by Nate Larkin (Thomas Nelson, 2007).

National Distributors

UK: (and countries not listed below)
CWR, Waverley Abbey House, Waverley Lane, Farnham, Surrey GU9 8EP.
Tel: (01252) 784700 Outside UK (+44) 1252 784700

AUSTRALIA: CMC Australasia, PO Box 519, Belmont, Victoria 3216.
Tel: (03) 5241 3288 Fax: (03) 5241 3290

CANADA: David C Cook Distribution Canada, PO Box 98, 55 Woodslee Avenue, Paris, Ontario
N3L 3E5. Tel: 1800 263 2664

GHANA: Challenge Enterprises of Ghana, PO Box 5723, Accra.
Tel: (021) 222437/223249 Fax: (021) 226227

HONG KONG: Cross Communications Ltd, 1/F, 562A Nathan Road, Kowloon.
Tel: 2780 1188 Fax: 2770 6229

INDIA: Crystal Communications, 10-3-18/4/1, East Marredpalli, Secunderabad – 500026,
Andhra Pradesh.
Tel/Fax: (040) 27737145

KENYA: Keswick Books and Gifts Ltd, PO Box 10242-00400, Nairobi.
Tel: (254) 20 312639/3870125

MALAYSIA: Salvation Book Centre (M) Sdn Bhd, 23 Jalan SS 2/64, 47300 Petaling Jaya, Selangor.
Tel: (03) 78766411/78766797 Fax: (03) 78757066/78756360

NEW ZEALAND: CMC Australasia, PO Box 303298, North Harbour, Auckland 0751.
Tel: 0800 449 408 Fax: 0800 449 049

NIGERIA: FBFM, Helen Baugh House, 96 St Finbarr's College Road, Akoka, Lagos.
Tel: (01) 7747429/4700218/825775/827264

PHILIPPINES: OMF Literature Inc, 776 Boni Avenue, Mandaluyong City.
Tel: (02) 531 2183 Fax: (02) 531 1960

SINGAPORE: Alby Commercial Enterprises Pte Ltd, 95 Kallang Avenue #04-00, AIS Industrial
Building, 339420. Tel: (65) 629 27238 Fax: (65) 629 27235

SOUTH AFRICA: Struik Christian Books, 80 MacKenzie Street, PO Box 1144, Cape Town 8000.
Tel: (021) 462 4360 Fax: (021) 461 3612

SRI LANKA: Christombu Publications (Pvt) Ltd., Bartleet House, 65 Braybrooke Place,
Colombo 2. Tel: (9411) 2421073/2447665

TANZANIA: CLC Christian Book Centre, PO Box 1384, Mkwepu Street, Dar es Salaam.
Tel/Fax: (022) 2119439

USA: David C Cook Distribution Canada, PO Box 98, 55 Woodslee Avenue, Paris, Ontario N3L
3E5, Canada. Tel: 1800 263 2664

ZIMBABWE: Word of Life Books (Pvt) Ltd, Christian Media Centre, 8 Aberdeen Road, Avondale,
PO Box A480 Avondale, Harare.
Tel: (04) 333355 or 091301188

For email addresses, visit the CWR website: www.cwr.org.uk

CWR is a Registered Charity – Number 294387

CWR is a Limited Company registered in England – Registration Number 1990308

Day and Residential Courses
Counselling Training
Leadership Development
Biblical Study Courses
Regional Seminars
Ministry to Women
Daily Devotionals
Books and Videos
Conference Centre

Trusted all Over the World

CWR HAS GAINED A WORLDWIDE reputation as a centre of excellence for Bible-based training and resources. From our headquarters at Waverley Abbey House, Farnham, England, we have been serving God's people for over 40 years with a vision to help apply God's Word to everyday life and relationships. The daily devotional *Every Day with Jesus* is read by nearly a million readers an issue in more than 150 countries, and our unique courses in biblical studies and pastoral care are respected all over the world. Waverley Abbey House provides a conference centre in a tranquil setting.

For free brochures on our seminars and courses, conference facilities, or a catalogue of CWR resources, please contact us at the following address:
CWR, Waverley Abbey House, Waverley Lane, Farnham, Surrey GU9 8EP, UK

Telephone: +44 (0)1252 784700
Email: mail@cwr.org.uk
Website: www.cwr.org.uk

CWR **Applying God's Word** *to everyday life and relationships*

More insights from our wealth of experience

The Waverley Abbey Insight Series brings together biblical understanding and practical advice to offer clear insight, teaching and help on a range of issues.

Insight into Anger – Learn how to diagnose the deep roots of inappropriate anger and discover how to overcome resentment, rage and bitterness.
ISBN: 978-1-85345-437-0 **£7.99**

Insight into Anxiety – Discover just what anxiety is, who is at risk of it and how to help those who suffer from it.
ISBN: 978-1-85345-436-3 **£7.99**

Insight into Forgiveness – Find freedom from the past through the power to forgive, and see how living a life of forgiveness brings release and freedom.
ISBN: 978-1-85345-491-2 **£7.99**

Insight into Perfectionism – Overcome pressures to look perfect, behave perfectly or perform tasks perfectly, and enjoy deep inner security, acceptance and rest.
ISBN: 978-1-85345-506-3 **£7.99**

Insight into Bereavement – Find out what emotions arise when a loved one dies, we experience divorce or the loss of a job etc, and learn how to work through the grieving process.
ISBN: 978-1-85345-385-4 **£7.50**

Insight into Eating Disorders – Discover the root causes of eating disorders and deal effectively with the denial and self-destruction that trap most sufferers. Written by a former anorexic and the founder of an eating disorders charity.
ISBN: 978-1-85345-410-3 **£7.50**

Insight into Self-esteem – Cultivate healthy self-esteem by deepening your relationship with God.
ISBN: 978-1-85345-409-7 **£7.50**

Insight into Stress – Recognise stress and its causes, and learn what you can do about it.
ISBN: 978-1-85345-384-7 **£7.50**

Prices correct at time of printing and exclude p&p

Available from CWR by calling **+44 (0)1252 784710**, online at **www.cwrstore.org.uk** – or from your local Christian bookshop.